"Most of us in the church have at one time or another been captivated by the mystery of the spiritual gift of tongues. This book will move the conversation forward in how we understand and engage with this most interesting gift of the Holy Spirit. Shel Boese is fresh, researched, and thoughtful, and I am most grateful for his contribution."

—**Bruxy Cavey**
Author of *End of Religion*

"Boese offers a bold contribution to the exciting field of contemporary Pentecostal theology. . . . Under Boese's insightful analysis, speaking in tongues—far from emerging as an academic embarrassment—is recognized as one of the 'foolish things' that confounds the worldly-wise: a divine gift that offers communal prophetic power wrapped in the appearance of weakness. As a fellow pastor-theologian, I highly recommend this book!"

—**Paul Rhodes Eddy**
Professor, Bethel University, and teaching pastor, Woodland Hills Church

"I found this work to be fascinating, creative, and a profound contribution to the field of both Pentecostal studies and postmodern thought. . . . A creative and persuasive argument and very well written. . . . Enjoyable to read for its contemporary relevance and uniqueness of argument."

—**Kyle Roberts**
Vice president, dean, and professor, United Theological Seminary of the Twin Cities

"Shelby Boese leads us down out of the ivory tower of theological intellectualism into the playground of spiritual awakening, where speaking in tongues can open the way for Spirit-led imagination, insight, and freedom. In a time when intellectual skepticism and ideological battles abound, Boese's insights provide a much-needed callback to a childlike relationship with God, and the importance of tongues to a disciple-making community."

—**Tim Day**
Author of *God Enters Stage Left*

"By attending to noncognitive dimensions of language, Boese reimagines 'speaking in tongues' as a gift of the Spirit which sustains 'play' for the purpose of mystic union, prophetic empowerment, and liberation. It is a creative and powerful reappropriation of the 'old line' Pentecostal/charismatic distinctive to reinvigorate the life and Spirit-led witness of the local church. Boese has important things to say to pastors and theologians alike, whether or not you claim the Pentecostal/charismatic tradition as your own."

—**David Williams**
President, Taylor Seminary

"We need a book that offers a fresh look at the gift of tongues as it relates to God's in-breaking kingdom over against the oppressive forces in our world today who seek to confine our imaginations. Few resources have offered a focused look at how this gift isn't some mere oddity in Christian faith, but integral to the church's formation in Christlikeness and mission. I hope to hold Shelby Boese's book in hand as a guide in these areas of Christian faith."

—**Kurt Willems**
Pastor, podcaster, and author of *Echoing Hope*

PLAY, TONGUES,

AND

LIBERATION POWER

PLAY, TONGUES,

AND

LIBERATION POWER

By
Shelby T. Boese

WIPF & STOCK · Eugene, Oregon

PLAY, TONGUES, AND LIBERATION POWER

Wipf & Stock
An Imprint of Wipf and Stock Publishers
199 W. 8th Ave., Suite 3
Eugene, OR 97401

www.wipfandstock.com

PAPERBACK ISBN: 978-1-7252-9207-9
HARDCOVER ISBN: 978-1-7252-9206-2
EBOOK ISBN: 978-1-7252-9208-6

04/30/21

Contents

Abstract

RECENT SCHOLARSHIP IS STARTING to pick up again regarding the practice of speaking in tongues. A decline had occurred as the mainline (old-line) charismatic movement waned in the 1990s. Today, however, the continued growth of the Pentecostal/charismatic, or renewalist, expressions of Christianity has brought these gifts back into focus. This thesis explores intersections between play as a primary pentecostal theological category and speaking in tongues. Furthermore it will explore how, as an expression of play, "tongues speech" acts as a sustaining gift which results in ongoing prophetic critique, empowerment, and liberation. Aspects of how the various dynamics of play possibly work in tongues are explored in more detail along with arguments for the re-invigoration of "tongues speech" in the teaching and gatherings of the local church.

Acknowledgments

As a full-time pastor this has been a slow process with many life interruptions, including church planting, site planting, two international moves, and serving three congregations. I wish to thank my wife, Anne Boese, who believed in me and encouraged me in various ways over the years to pursue new things; and my children, who have been sources of joy and who also have wondered why on earth I am still in school.

I also wish to acknowledge the faculty, former and present, at United, for their teaching, openness, and encouragement. Jean Trumbauer, Sharon Tan, and Kyle Roberts in particular have been vital in these roles.

A big thanks to Loretta Tschetter for editing work and helping me work toward clarity.

The congregations I have the joy of serving. First Assembly of God Christian Center/Sioux Falls First, Sioux Falls, South Dakota; Mercy Church (Christian & Missionary Alliance/Mennonite Church), Sioux Falls, South Dakota; The Meetinghouse (Be In Christ, BIC Canada)—High Park Parish, Toronto, Ontario; Bay Shore (Mennonite) Church, Sarasota, Florida; Pilgrim Church, Vancouver, British Columbia; for calling a pastor with many different interests in the richness of the kingdom of God.

My grandfather, Glen Boese (farmer, teacher, missionary, freedom rider), of blessed memory, whose passion and example for the kingdom of God, Jesus, and justice continue to inspire me.

Acknowledgments

Finally, being a Pentecostal-Anabaptist, I must name Jesus. He who is living and active by the Holy Spirit. May many continue to find and be found by him.

Introductory Notes

THE BACKGROUND FOR THIS thesis stems from my personal and pastoral experiences, as well as a lack of constructive theological reflection and work on the gift of speaking in tongues, or a more generic term "ecstatic speech," in Christian practice.[1] Pentecostals, who generally practice this gift, are still very much coming of age in the academy. The earliest scholars assumed a position within their own communities, then second-generation pentecostal scholars such as Gordon Fee established interpretive grids within mainline Evangelicalism, and now we see the wider theological community of scholars looking at Pentecostalism from outside, while pentecostal scholars, in turn, engage the wider theological community from within. I believe that some in this generation gave up too much unique epistemological and hermeneutical ground to modernistic, evangelical, academic assumptions and did not emphasize unique perspectives on theology that flow out of pentecostal experience. Martin Mittelstadt articulates three phases of Pentecostal scholarship and provides good analysis of the past evangelical pitfalls of Pentecostal theology.[2]

1. Ecstatic speech. I will use the terms "speaking in tongues," "ecstatic speech," "tongues," and "tongues speech" interchangeably to refer to glosso-lalic speech for human and non-human unlearned languages by the speaker. I am aware of some debate about the technical use of "ecstatic speech" if that is meant to express tongues speech as only occurring in a state of ecstasy. My intention in using this term is based more upon the observer's position than the speaker's actual state, which is generally a state of play, which may overlap with ecstasy.

2. Mittelstadt, *Reading Luke-Acts*, 12–16.

More pointedly, the unique implications and functions of "tongues speech" on the role and use of language have not been adequately explored. The next generations are doing better, in part because postmodernism and deconstructionism have entered into the theological discourse more.[3] Some very recent examples of this pentecostal scholarship come from James K. A. Smith, Martin W. Mittelstadt, and others. Through this work I desire to add a pastoral-theologian voice to the conversation. As a developing pastor theologian, I am adding my voice to this conversation to engage in the task of Mittelstadt's challenge (following) to use this opportunity opening up for Pentecostals in a shifting local and global context.

> While many Western Christians, particularly those closely associated with the Evangelical and fundamentalist movements, demand that the world maintain the assumptions of modernism simply because they have canonized them,
>
> Pentecostalism, also part of the cultural shifts occurring through the world, stands at an axis of prime opportunity. Theology and ideological paradigms in place for centuries need to be rethought, removed or recreated not in an effort towards trendiness, but contextually to an ever-evolving, pluralistic world.[4]

The other reality that leads me in this direction is the number of indigenous churches in the majority world who more naturally embrace the phenomenon of gifts of the Spirit, and "tongues speech" in particular, even though some do not use the descriptors "pentecostal/charismatic." This reality points to my central thesis that speaking in tongues is the gift which sustains play, mystical union, prophetic empowerment, and liberation.

---

3. Mittelstadt, *Reading Luke-Acts*, 14–16.
4. Mittelstadt, *Reading Luke-Acts*, 145–46.

Presuppositions

1. The use of the word "pentecostal." I use the word "pentecostal" in a broad, inclusive sense. This inclusive sense encompasses not only denominational Pentecostals, nor simply those who see speaking tongues as the initial physical evidence (to abbreviate: IPE doctrine of tongues) of subsequent infilling or baptism of the Holy Spirit. It would include, for example, those who practice charismatic gifts but would not affirm the IPE doctrine (in any form), nor necessarily the doctrine of subsequence with all who welcome the gifts of the Holy Spirit in church life. My use of the word "pentecostal" would be similar to Yong's "Renewalist" term and in agreement with Smith's use of the word with a lowercase "p" to indicate this broad sense.

2. The Christian story as presented in the New Testament Luke-Acts is rooted in historical realities. I have an inspirationist-based "high view" of Scripture. In this I am personally guided by the Mennonite Confession of Faith (1995).[5] The high view in this instance means that Scripture is the norming norm without getting into the various meanings of the use of terms such as "inspired," "inerrant," "infallible," or "authoritative," which all take on different meanings depending on the group. I can affirm these terms under certain understandings that include the starting point of affirming divine revelation through inspired writers using inspired and varied genres that are not all to be taken literally, but rather according to literary type.

3. The growth of global church, which is largely charismatic. I presume the reader is aware of the global and explosive

---

5. "Article 4—We believe that all Scripture is inspired by God through the Holy Spirit for instruction in salvation and training in righteousness. We accept the Scriptures as the Word of God and as the fully reliable and trustworthy standard for Christian faith and life. Led by the Holy Spirit in the church, we interpret Scripture in harmony with Jesus Christ" ("Confession of Faith in a Mennonite Perspective").

growth of Charismatic practices in all Protestant Christian churches, even within those that do not officially acknowledge, affirm, or welcome such practices in their Western, privileged-world contexts. For example the UCC has been joined by pentecostal groups such as The Fellowship.[6] While I will not be rehashing the research on this, it is part of the need for more writing on the subject.

4. The use of language central to communication. Language conveys meaning. While this may seem superfluous to point out, the power of language cannot be understated. It is the glue of society. There are many debates about how meaning is conveyed and the performative aspects of language; however, what has not been explored enough from a pentecostal standpoint is the radical nature of language that performs but does not do so because of conveyance of meaning in any clearly ordered, cognitive way.

"Tongues speech" has a prophetic function as identified by many pentecostal scholars, such as Roger Stronstad and Glen Menzies. The prophetic function is Holy Spirit–inspired speech that brings the gospel of the kingdom through the scandal of Jesus to bear through specific people, times, and places. My goal is to explore more fully the depth of this prophetic function. Specifically, the inherent critique of language and also the result of this power mediated through the means of "tongues speech" will be more fully articulated in my thesis. Power as a spiritual working or energy will be explored and defined in the Lukan use, which results in bold proclamation of Jesus and perseverance in the face of persecution from majorities.

"Tongues speech" provides direct prophetic spiritual empowerment by giving, calling, and causing people to play with language. As such, ecstatic speech is the original, unmediated, and untamable force that both deconstructs human control through language and is a stroke of empowerment. It produces personal and corporate solidarity against the centralizing cultural structures

---

6. Brekke, Review of *Signs and Wonders*.

of division by ethnicity, class, gender, and socioeconomic status. It therefore has something to contribute to human flourishing as an ongoing decentering speech of resistance and liberation. Peter the apostle, in Acts 2, quoting from the prophet Joel indicates that this inspired speech is that which tears down walls between the marginalized and the center. "Tongues speech" leads to prophetic speech in known languages by first empowering through the direct experience of nonrational prayer (Cf. 1 Cor 14:2, 4, 14, 18, 39).

The "untamable" part will be emphasized in terms of the theology of direct empowerment around the means of control entailed in the uses of language. This is where postmodernisms meet up with Jesus' Spirit.[7] "Tongues speech" turns all who will receive it into walking parables and prophets through language as an act of prophetic denunciation meets performance art. For those on the margins it leapfrogs the normal barriers to power put up through those who control the discourse and sense of knowledge via language. For the empowered it brings a humility and also exposes the "idolatry of language"[8] and causes a solidarity with the other (whoever is not in the culturally empowered group) by entering into parabolic speech that by its very nature is not the language of the powerful since it cannot be used to control.

An additional goal will be to encourage churches of all kinds to welcome and "seek earnestly" the spiritual gifts, with a Lukan emphasis on language gifts (which display a different kind of coherence and power), and most particularly the gifts of speaking in tongues (glossolalia).[9] This encouragement will be part of the

7. Postmodernism: I am using Jean-François Lyotard's well-known definition in *The Postmodern Condition*, xxiv–xxv: "Simplifying to the extreme, I define postmodernism as incredulity towards metanarratives"—a suspicion of, often with deconstruction of, large stories that provide coherent meaning, including secular theories.

8. "Idolatry of language" is a term borrowed from liberationist-feminist theologian Rosemary Radford Ruether. My use, however, is expanded to include all language which always has exclusionary aspects to the marginalized, not simply the problem of God-language and gender.

9. Spiritual gifts: what Paul identifies as *charismata* or *pneumatika* in 1 Cor. 12, 13, and 14. Not simply natural talents developed or acquired skills, but those which are direct, empowered giftings of the Holy Spirit to members of

above theological construction with the pastoral theology of embracing otherness of the Holy Spirit, which will lead one to enter the otherness of those bound by structural and spiritual forces of brokenness. This is the work of the Spirit to empower and to make whole those on the margins, as Luke emphasizes as part and parcel of the Spirit-filled ministry of Jesus and the early church.

Summary

In this short work I will seek to explore, and sometimes draw out, the intersections between "tongues speech" (speaking in tongues) and empowerment, particularly how speaking in tongues is sustaining speech for play, mystical encounter, and prophetic imagination. My primary audience is the Pentecostal/Charismatic pastor who desires more tools to teach about and lead others into receiving the spiritual gift of speaking in tongues. I would argue anecdotally and from personal experience in various faith communities that this gift tends be marginalized where it is most needed and not reflected upon where it is most active.

The thesis is that speaking in tongues is a primary gift for sustaining prophetic empowerment and liberating play. It is seen as "a useless gift," yet its apparent foolishness results in great strength over models of strength and power in the anti-kingdom and non-play life. The intersections of speaking in tongues with play and the prophetic will be the bulk of the work. To summarize, speaking in tongues is the sustaining gift of play, mystical union, and prophetic liberating empowerment.

Speaking in tongues is a liberation-sustaining language. It liberates by awaking and sustaining the imagination through new speech that seizes against controlled, hegemonic speech of one's cultural bounds and imperial universal claims at the same time. Another way to speak of on-ramps into the freedom of liberation is the concept of the prophetic. Prophetic speech is that which exposes, deconstructs, and also employs hope through the speaking

---

the church or which take natural talents into another dimension of effectiveness for the mission of God.

of an alternative vision of life: it is a different way of naming reality and possibility. Speaking in tongues affects multiple layers of total-izing claims at the same time. However, the speaker is often not immediately aware of this, nor the critic of "tongues speech."

Process

I will be using a constructive theological process employing a sur-vey of some current writings on my subject. Primary conversation partners will include Walter Brueggemann and Jean-Jacques Su-urmond. In the case of Suurmond, I will primarily be referencing his work *Word and Spirit at Play, Towards a Charismatic Theol-ogy*. While this thesis will include some reference to philosophical theology of language, my primary mode of argumentation will be from Pentecostal theological sources. As part of this I will also be using a pentecostal hermeneutic.

The pentecostal academic hermeneutical approach I will use privileges the ministry of Jesus and particularly the Luke-Acts narratives. This hermeneutic is additionally shaped and informed by the experience and interplay (or just "play") of (1) the word (Protestant canon), (2) the Spirit within, and (3) the community (local churches).[10] Luke-Acts provides an interpretive and norm-ing framework for reading Scripture, interpreting the whole of Scripture, and experiential expectations. The experiences of the early church as relayed in Luke-Acts are considered normative for pentecostal expectations of being Christian and living as church.

As an aside, I am not concerned with reviewing the Pente-costal reading of Luke-Acts as a theologically intentional narra-tive regarding the charismatic ministry of the Holy Spirit. I take as a given what Stronstad names as a "hermeneutic of affirmation" regarding Luke's narratival intention: "This hermeneutic of af-firmation also affirms that Luke intends this paradigm about the pouring out of the Spirit of prophecy to extend to all believers, for he has reported Peter to announce, 'For the promise [that you shall

10. Vondey, *Beyond Pentecostalism*, 66.

receive the gift of the Holy Spirit] is for you and your children, and for all who are far off' (Acts 2:39)."[11] Volumes have been written on this and also a possible Johannine synthesis of Luke and Paul. Luke-Acts are assumed as models for contemporary behavior, particularly as relates to power for the mission of God. That is beyond the scope of this paper.[12]

It is important to note that there has been a historic anti-intellectualism of Pentecostalism. Modern Pentecostal students and academics have discussed overcoming this without capitulating entirely to the Western enlightenment captivity of much of the Western Christian academy. The first generation gave too much ground. I would go in another direction and say that the impulse towards anti-intellectualism of the early Pentecostals was grounded in their experience of the Spirit and the lack of language in the Western church of the day to give voice to their concerns. However, the Eastern Orthodox Church was not so mystically challenged, nor captive to enlightenment categories, in its understanding of theology. Indeed, the Eastern Orthodox Church saved my Pentecostalism from Western Evangelical hegemony. Lossky writes, "Christian Theology is always in the last resort a mean: a unit of knowledge subserving an end which transcends all knowledge. This ultimate end is union with god or deification, the *theosis* of the Greek Fathers."[13] The word for speaking in tongues, *Glossolalia*, is from the Greek root *glossai* ("tongues") and "was used of ancient or esoteric languages."[14] "Glossolalia" does not convey propositional content if left uninterpreted or transmuted. However, it does "do" something as this paper's focus is on certain aspects of its trans-rational speech with an iconoclastic purpose.[15]

---

11. Stronstad, *Prophethood*, 22.

12. Warrington, *Pentecostal Theology*, 104. Mittelstadt, *Reading Luke-Acts*, 91.

13. Lossky, *Mystical Theology*, 9.

14. Witherington, *Conflict and Community in Corinth*, 258.

15. McQueen, *Joel and the Spirit*, 100.

Layout of Arguments

In keeping with the character of play, my approach is more a weaving than a linear argument. There is enough order to jump in, but there is also doubling back and the picking up of new players. In chapter 1 I will define speaking in tongues, also referred to as "tongues speech." This will involve sketching connections between "tongues speech" and imagination. In chapter 2 I will build on play as a primary Pentecostal theological lens and explore it as a central way of understanding speaking in tongues as empowerment and prophetic catalyst. We will also develop theories of how speaking in tongues empowers through imagination. This power is essentially liberative on a personal and corporate level. In chapter 3 we will engage a practical theology of cultivating "tongues speech" and holy imagination.

For ministry I strongly affirm and see this work as one aspect of Warrington's plea, "Guidance needs to be offered to acquaint Pentecostals with the value and relevance of this gift to their ongoing development as believers for it is a gift from God intended to 'become the "occasion" for a new theophany and a new level of intimacy with God.'"[16]

---

16. Warrington, *Pentecostal Theology*, 95; Chan, *Pentecostal Theology*, 78.

CHAPTER 1

Speaking in Tongues as Imaginative Prophetic Empowerment

1.1 Defining Tongues Speech for the Unfamiliar

KEITH WARRINGTON IS WORTH quoting at length here:

> The gift of tongues is best understood as an extemporaneous or spontaneous manifestation in a form that is a quasi-language. The speaker is in control of her/his speech and the forming of sounds; the Spirit does not manipulate or coerce the speaker into a particular speech pattern. It is possible that the sounds themselves already existed in the mind and experience of the speaker, being reconstituted in the form of the tongues s/he employs though it also possible that they are previously unimagined phonetic forms. Most Pentecostals have concluded that speaking in tongues is a phenomenon that has divine and human elements in that the Spirit inspires the manifestation but the person articulates the sounds.[1]

The primary biblical texts that speak directly about "tongues speech" include 1 Cor 12:10, 30, 14:4, 13–22, 27, 28. The content

1. Warrington, *Pentecostal Theology*, 87.

of "tongues speech" when interpreted seems to be prayer or praise directed to God or a message to believers or unbelievers. The New Testament texts do not exclude the message in tongues directed to other persons. The act of interpretation may not be, and most assuredly in many experiences is not, simply a direct translation. Rather the interpretation can be an act of prophetic speech, inspired by the prayer in tongues. The New Testament texts regarding the operation of the Spiritual gifts generally are understood to be expansive and more concerned about their operation under the Law of Love (1 Cor 13) since they are not character-development dependent.[2] To restate, "tongues speech" is first and foremost a mystical embodied encounter with God. In reference to 1 Cor 14:2, Menzies states, "Paul can use the term 'mystery' to refer to specific aspects of God's redemptive plan. . . . Here, the term simply 'carries . . . the sense of that which lies outside the understanding for the speaker and hearer.'"[3] This speaking, enabled by God and transmitted through the speaker back to God, makes little sense except also as a form of mystical union and relationship as gift. "It is an objective spiritual reality, not to be applied in the same manner as establishing church government, the Lord's Supper, nor undergoing water baptism."[4] This language is Spirit-filled. It is not language in an ordinary sense because it communicates in neither a direct, colloquial way nor in a formal manner.

Speaking in tongues is also referred to by Paul as praying and praising (doxological use of tongues) in "my spirit" in 1 Cor 14:14. "Spirit" is language for the nonrational aspect of humanness. Paul values and practices both praying "in my spirit" and with "my mind."[5] Prayer is the center of all true theology and experience in Pentecostal spirituality, and praying in tongues or "tongues speech" is at its heart God oriented. Speaking in tongues within traditional Pentecostal circles is both an initial evidence of Spirit empowerment and an ongoing aspect of empowering prayer that will open

2. Warrington, *Pentecostal Theology,* 94.

3. Fee, *Corinthians,* 656. Quoted, Menzies, *Speaking in Tongues,* 130–31.

4. Stronstad, *Prophethood,* 26.

5. Witherington, *Conflict and Community,* 282.

a person to receiving whatever other gift is needed to advance the mission of God.[6] I will go beyond this by arguing that the nature of this empowerment for mission, or "sustaining power," involves mystical union, play, and liminality and is inherently prophetic, giving it a sanctifying aspect. In short, the "least of these gifts," a non-biblical phrase reading 1 Cor 12:31 back onto tongues only, is more than a "gateway" gift as some Pentecostals have been taught; it is the spiritual participation (synergism) and union with the primordial Word of creation.

There are at least three prophetic moves in speaking in tongues: (1) The chosen participation of the individual to seek, receive, and use the gift requires an inwardly directed prophetic critique of one's own personal use of language and desire to control. Personal power is checked by a humility that dethrones the personal "idolatry of language" and even one's own thoughts. (2) A prophetic move of critiquing the cultural hegemony that is inherent in any language by simply revealing the captivity of any given language and its limits. (3) A prophetic move which empowers new speech in and through the person, using their known communicative languages after, and while, coming out of "tongues speech" "playtimes" into non-play life.

1.2 Speaking in New Tongues as Playful Prophetic Imaginative Empowerment

And these signs will accompany those who believe: In my name they will drive out demons; they will speak in new tongues.

—MARK 16:17

Speaking in tongues is empowering and liberating play that one enters into as a gift of the Holy Spirit. "Tongues speech" as empowering and liberating is not a new thought. Here we want to zoom in on the possible aspects of *how* this speech liberates, empowers, and calls. Keeping in mind the very nature of the gift of

---

6. Menzies and Menzies, *Spirit and Power*, 117.

tongues keeps us from idolizing "how" questions in our relationship with God. For the privileged as well as the empowered its play is idol-smashing.[7] How, or by what means, does it call the church continually (if practiced) into a renewed vision, which empowers action of God's kingdom as expressed in the life, teachings, death, and resurrection of Jesus? Luke's Gospel articulates this call to be a charismatic community until the King returns.[8] A continually renewed vision of another way of being in the world is the why and how of the "least" of the spiritual gifts, speaking in tongues.

It is my contention that *speaking in tongues guards and sustains the centrality of play* and its empowering aspects. Speaking in tongues is a gift that best sustains play, mystical union, prophetic empowerment, and liberation. Play is a central aspect to what speaking in tongues is and the kind of prophetic activity it results in directly and indirectly with language. Play is both structured and unstructured and grants the experience of liminality. Liminality is "a kind of anti-structure in which profane social relationships are set aside, rights and obligations are suspended, and participants engage in the sacred in complex episodes of sacred space-time through subversive, playful events. This anti-structure is capable of storing alternative models of reality that can influence mainstream (non-play) social structure and therefore direct social change."[9]

The furniture we want to place in the room of this discussion of speaking in tongues would be that of play, mystical union, and the prophetic. "To have the Spirit of YHWH is to be empowered" is the very promise of the prophet Joel to the Judean people, who were weak, powerless, and helpless. So this word is the main interpretive text for the pouring out of the Spirit in the New Testament. Joel's prophecy also hints at the future of the New Testament glossolalic event as an empowerment that bring inclusion for all people, which begins wholesale in Acts 10:44–47. Privileges of power and access are opened to all by the work of the Spirit.[10]

7. Suurmond, *Word and Spirit*, 30.

8. Stronstad, *Charismatic Theology*, 69.

9. Althouse, "Betwixt and Between," 268.

10. Macchia, *Justified*, 33.

Simon Chan and Wolfgang Vondey, in *Beyond Pentecostalism*, as well as Jean-Jacques Suurmond and others, emphasize the role of play in pentecostal theology.

Reflecting on Steven Land's orthopathy, which is an action-reflection movement of pentecostal worship, Vondey tells us that "improvisation . . . points to the importance of integrating orthodoxy and orthopraxy with orthopathy." Holy imagination is the place of play of the Holy Spirit. It is "in the play of the imagination, theology expands to the realm of the good, the holy, and the beautiful that enter the world through visions, dreams, and prophecies—habits of orthopathy that are the objective, relational, and dispositional operations of the Holy Spirit in the Christian life."[11] The play of the Spirit involves the imagination and Christ-centered use of art in worship as the main sources of theophanic encounter. Vondey says, "The freedom of play is a significant aspect of Pentecostalism; it emphasizes that theological pursuit cannot be pure performance. In play, there is no audience; it is not a dramatic act but an invitation to participate in a shared corporeal, spiritual, intellectual, and ethical celebration. . . . Play is not aimed at a performance to 'non–players'; it is interested in playing *with* others, not *for* others."[12] Chan summarizes both Huizinga and Suurmond's broad definition of play, and we might see this as our working definition of play: "an occasion when people choose to suspend the ordinary course of life to enter into a world of free spontaneous relationships. . . . Play creates order, is order. Into an imperfect world and into the confusion of life it brings a temporary, a limited perfection."[13] As we will see, "order" is a bit problematic, unless understood as a state of affairs of thriving in opposition to "control." This is an important distinction. Play involves freedom and order that allows the players to enter a space where they can thrive independent of non-play life and circumstances. In that thriving they are liberated and empowered. Speaking in tongues is perhaps

11. Vondey, *Beyond Pentecostalism*, 44.

12. Vondey, *Beyond Pentecostalism*, 43.

13. Chan, *Pentecostal Theology*, 116–17.

the freest form of play possible.[14] "Within the world of play, new understandings of life are discovered, new relationships are forged, we return from the world of play better able to deal with the challenge of ordinary 'living.'"[15] Peter Althouse affirms this: "Ritual [worship gathering] play is a lens through which an understanding of the varieties of Pentecostal worship is particularly salient for understanding Pentecostal ritual in a way that bridges both scientific and theological analyses."[16]

The game or context of play also has boundaries. One enters into and out of play, there is play and non-play life. This can be spoken of in terms of liminality, which we shall do later. The more playful one is, the more easily they access their imaginative faculties in non-play life—crossing back and forth. "Limitations (both in rules and in the nature of the players) are essential for a game and give it its challenge, tension and integrity. Only finite, limited beings can therefore play. . . . On the other hand the infinite God can play only in and through finite creatures."[17]

I use in part Walter Brueggemann's definition of imagination, "*imagine*, that is to utter, entertain, describe, and construe a world other than the one that is manifest in front of us . . . the offer of prophetic imagination is one that contradicts the taken-for-granted world around us."[18] Regarding the spoken word, Brueggemann says, "Prophetic preaching is an effort to imagine the world as though YHWH, the creator of heaven and earth, the Father of our Lord Jesus Christ whom we name as Father, Son, and Spirit, is a real character and the defining agent in the world."[19]

In this regard "tongues speech" is an imagination awakening and sustaining speech. Speaking in tongues is imaginative, beyond or against the given realities of the world and speaker, by directly contradicting the most fundamental ways in which the world is

14. Suurmond, *Word and Spirit at Play*, 31.

15. Chan, *Pentecostal Theology*, 117.

16. Althouse, "Betwixt and Between," 266.

17. Suurmond, *Word and Spirit*, 122.

18. Brueggemann, *Practice of Prophetic Imagination*, 2, 25.

19. Brueggemann, *Practice of Prophetic Imagination*, 71.

ordered and controlled through speech and naming. This would be congruent with Smith's challenge for pentecostals to think beyond the existing naturalistic furniture in the room because our ontology is making different claims of what is.[20] So there is, at one level, imaginative language that undermines enlightenment assumptions about what is really real, though it's nonsensical in nature. Then, at a different (but interconnected way in the play) level, the view of selfhood is altered. Cosmic and hyper-localized imagination is activated and opened up to receive new knowledge and experience beyond the person's view of what is.

Imagination as place of encounter and liberation through "tongues speech" can also be thought of in more classic Pentecostal terms as stated by Stronstad. He relates that Spirit-baptism (in the classical Pentecostal sense with tongues as sign) leads to sign, wonder, and witness. In the traditioning of Spirit-baptism in a counter-cultural Pentecostal community, a new expectation is created for life, which can result in the reenchantment bringing the freedom to imagine anew, leading to liberation.[21]

Speaking in tongues is a speech that can come before and keep critiquing, while empowering the prophetic speech of the church and individual. "Tongues speech is a manifestation of prophetic inspiration." It is an eschatological language longing for *complete* fulfillment of salvation.[22] It is prophetic empowerment that begins with dismantling speech as a method of control. Its first move is to call the individual, and then the church that makes space for this gift, to relinquishment. The speech act of speaking in tongues creates a decisive break, both in the person praying and in the person hearing, from other controlled uses of speech. It is nonsense to the kingdom of the world speech which seeks to deny God's work.

This gift functions as an intentional *partialing* of language, opening space for future wholeness. First Corinthians 13:8–10 makes the case that the word gifts such as prophecy and speaking in tongues function as partial aspects of knowledge and experience

20. Smith, *Thinking in Tongues*, 97.

21. Stronstad, *Prophethood*, 77.

22. Macchia, *Justified*, 44.

in the penultimate expression of the Spirit in the individual, church, and world.

That "tongues speech" entails a partial aspect of common language use makes it a pointer beyond itself and summons other suppressed faculties of knowing and experience such as imagination in Spirit-oriented play in worship. The gifts of the Spirit require such play in order to be in operation in a person and faith community.

Speaking in tongues is itself prophetic in that it critiques normal speech and language as a means of control. It is not prophetic communication in the sense of an understandable language to another using normal sign/signified designations. In this sense it is preprophetic, a prophetic breaking of the given speech of a culture or hegemon, with empowerment leading to possible prophetic speech within a culture. I am meaning "prophetic speech" in both senses of (1) a uniquely Spirit-inspired message in the common language of the person(s), and (2) in the critique of language by the very practice of speaking in tongues against the language of empire, status-quo power structures, and injustice. Menzies as well argues that "a close reading of Luke's narrative reveals that he views speaking in tongues as a special type of prophetic speech" in his analysis of Acts 2:17–18, 19:6, 10:42–48.[23] Speaking in tongues creates space for new imagination. It is guaranteed to be truthful because it is not controlled by imperial or cultural cognitive weight.

Let's start with the latter. Speaking in tongues provides an inherent prophetic critique of language itself as a means of order and control. This spiritual gift most distinguishes pentecostalism from Evangelicalism. While some would say that Paul forbids speaking in tongues in the public assembly with criterion being intelligibility and edification of others, this does not do full justice to the kind of sign people praying in tongues together embodies and produces. It is also a narrowing of intelligibility to mean shared common language.[24]

23. Menzies, *Speaking in Tongues*, 19.
24. Witherington, *Conflict and Community*, 281.

Such prayer together is a shared experience (as will we say is play) that may not be intelligible in a straightforward way. A group looking at a visual art piece may not be communicating with one another "intelligibly" but they can walk away and speak about what the piece has done and is doing in them individually, and then together they may form new perspectives. At its heart, classical Pentecostalism contains a postmodern sensibility (this is in spite of what many on-the-street pentecostals would claim, since they are mostly getting their descriptive language for faith from the place where the line between fundamentalism and Evangelicalism is being blurred)—an incredulity towards the metanarrative of language itself. There is an amazing act of deconstruction of language in its normal usage. In the same stroke there is an "experiential unification—the pentecostal edge" in the practice of speaking in tongues.[25]

Another way to speak of this is that speaking in tongues is sacramental. It brings the speaker(s) and hearer(s) into a liminal experience. Sacraments call forth faith because they are literally unbelievable and beyond expectation. Symbols can bridge or block experience; "tongues speech" can be understood as having sacramental import because it breaks the normal signifying use of language.[26] Suurmond in speaking of rites of worship in the church says, "By contrast, if they [rites] remain living and serve the liturgical game, then—like parables, humor, glossolalia [speaking in tongues] and the foolishness of other charismatic expressions—for a moment they take us out of our automatic way of living in accordance with the order of this world and open us to the possibilities of the Kingdom of God."[27]

Imagination in the Pentecostal practice moves beyond only reconfigured sense perception experiences and imitation. It is also a seat of encounter with the Holy Spirit. It is a path to the transcendent and the divine. Vondey states, "The revival of imagination among Pentecostals and its oral, affectionate expression in

25. Noel, *Pentecostal and Postmodern Hermeneutics*, 164.

26. Macchia, *Justified*, 286.

27. Suurmond, *Word and Spirit* 87.

tongues clearly exposed the crisis of imagination in the late modern world."[28] This imagination leads to an outward expression of the vision of God for the world. It is not simply about an interior experience but leads into a new vision of life. This is the holy and end-oriented (eschatological) aspect, hence "holy imagination" which leads to a more focused "prophetic imagination." The prophetic imagination is opened into and expanded upon via direct experiences and practices of play, such as "tongues speech."

> To qualify "prophetic" by "imagination" is to dig deeper than moved earnestness into the notion of playful, venturesome probing into the unknown that requires poetic utterance and that evokes daring images and metaphors, all in the service of an illusiveness out beyond royal totalism. To evade royal totalism requires an emancipated imagination that refuses the domesticated categories of settled control.[29]

The prophetic imagination grants an alternative to the cultural and imperial hegemonic claims on the world, community of faith, and individual. It pushes against atheism and other theisms. Here is where we see empowerment through the use of it. This is essential to my claim of freedom through the practice of spiritual gifts and of speaking in tongues in particular. This speech grants an alternative mode of power and access to prophetic imagination and speech. This is another way the biblical text becomes accessible to one who has no other educational or institutional access. Charismatic gifts make spiritual wisdom known to outsiders of the kingdom of God. "The Spirit puts us in a position to think God's deepest thoughts (1 Cor 2:10–12), in other words God's 'hidden wisdom' which chooses those who are 'of no account' in this world to manifest all the more clearly the unconditional character of grace, so that 'there is no room for boasting before God' (1:29)."[30]

Whether through the church or academy, the direct empowerment of the Spirit does not need to play by any other language

28. Vondey, *Beyond Pentecostalism*, 31.

29. Brueggemann, *Practice of Prophetic Imagination*, 22.

30. Suurmond, *Word and Spirit*, 51.

games. This mode through the Spirit is granted when there is not another choice in configuring life and the stories that one lives in, where there is no freedom, nor awareness of one's bondage to a current system of knowing, being, and doing life. "Meaning in the Pentecostal story depends neither on the ability of the mind to conceptualize nor on the capacity of language to express it as truth. Instead, the Pentecostal imagination is an invitation to experience God's Spirit despite these human limitations."[31]

"Tongues speech" helps enable one to enter into practice of prophetic imagination because the moment one utters a tongue they begin a journey of entering play as a liminal place. It collapses the normal time needed to enter into a liminal place required often in aesthetic-only approaches to play. Althouse again, "Liminality is connected to ritual play in that liminal play employs the subjunctive ('as if') mood rather than the indicative ('as is') mood. . . . In the context of Pentecostal worship the subjunctive is engaged in . . . [and] remembers the redemptive life and work of Christ 'as if' it is tangible reality in the present and hopes for the coming eschatological day 'as if' the Spirit is already making its dawning a reality."[32] Of all aspects of play that bring one into a liminal state, speaking in tongues creates the most immediate break possible with non-play, pre-/post-liminal life and experience. The first syllable uttered in "tongues speech" is immediate entrance into play, and therefore this gift is of vital importance to sustaining the power, liberation, and experience of the grace of God in life.

This kind of speech obviously deconstructs the normal linguistic acts. Speaking in tongues is a kind of ironic iconoclasm of language. When one is so captive to culture, swimming in the precepts, lies, and vocabulary of one's empire, speaking in tongues starts to chip away at that hegemon. Other ways to name this hegemony include that which is against the law of love in Christ (John 1:17; 1 John 4:7–8; Matt 22:37–39) and also named as the kingdom of the world or the darkness. Put around another way it is speech of negation. All uses of language that seek to order the world devoid

31. Vondey, *Beyond Pentecostalism*, 34.
32. Althouse, "Betwixt and Between," 266–67.

of God are exposed in ecstatic speech. This is its first prophetic move regardless of the speaker's or hearer's intentions. Therefore there is power of liberation in every sound made which cannot be named. It is ironic in that speaking in tongues turns a person into an icon of sound in the religious sense. An "icon"is "expression through a material medium of the divine realities—symbol and pledge of our sanctification,"[33] Lossky writes about the icon in the Eastern Orthodox Church. Without a detailed dive into the theology of the icon, it bears some superficial parallels to "tongues speech" in that it is turning sound into art that is a symbolic representation of the ineffable nature of God's ultimate being. In this way it sustains personal experience of the mystery and incarnation in a holy tension by the very Spirit of God. It is sheer grace revelation. Speaking in tongues in a limited way (indeed, all is limited) gives us a personal experience of the infinite and incomprehensible God. That is, "all that is comprehensible about Him is His infinity and incomprehensibility."[34] Speaking in tongues is a gift that emphasizes to us the denial of language and its limits in our experience of God, while simultaneously providing access to mystical union. Play is a Western way to also speak of this.

When you are a fish in the river of Babylon it's hard to see the water. How do you un-drink the Kool-Aid of language and linguistic hegemony which rules the very thoughts and imagination you have been immersed in? Visual art has some capacity to do this when you observe it. Music has the same capacity, but it is still bound to a large extent to speech. The turn to Babel in "tongues speech" is able to do this while critiquing language in same stroke. "Tongues speech" is destructuring and reconstituting in a way not accessible to the taming of empire. "Dominant 'word-making' and 'world-making' are always in the hands of those who control technology, word-versions of reality are regularly the word of the strong against the weak." The promise that "they shall speak with

---

33. Lossky, *Mystical Theology*, 10, 25.
34. Lossky, *Mystical Theology*, 36.

new tongues" is one of truthful speech that has been emptied of religious domestication and is now creating a new world.[35]

It is also of note that we see in the growing persecuted church a strong charismatic element, whether under the old USSR or present communist China. "The impact of Pentecostal belief and praxis upon the contemporary Chinese church should not surprise us. The Azusa Street Revival (1906–1909), the key catalyst of the movement, was still burning brightly when its first representatives arrived in Hong Kong in 1907. The Pentecostal message quickly spread to other parts of China and had an immediate impact. Indeed, one of the striking aspects of Christianity in pre–1949 China was the emergence of strong, vital indigenous churches. These churches were founded and led by Chinese Christians. They were established and operated entirely independent of foreign finances, control, and leadership. Two of the three largest independent Chinese churches that sprang up in the early part of the twentieth century were Pentecostal."[36] "Tongues speech" as central to the growth of the church in hard places has always been the norm. It is an empowering speech that cannot be "listened in on" with the purpose of learning the content and preempting the issues or controlling them. There is no access for the would-be hegemon to the speech. The empowerment cannot be thwarted by other powers.[37] Speaking in tongues empowers by answering to all that the impossible is where God breaks in and in doing this also encourages both speaker and hearer (even the one hearing their own speech). It gives language to newness as a gift of God against the impossible. It is impossible speech which channels the primordial language of creation.[38]

35. Brueggemann, *Word Militant,* 171.

36. Menzies, "Pentecostal Theology."

37. Albert, "Christianity in China."

38. Brueggemann, *Practice of Prophetic Imagination,* 96, 106.

1.3 Sustaining Play and Imagination

Speaking in tongues is prophetic or preprophetic play. As speech that is beyond prophetic-cognitive type it brings an emotive and artistic critique of language. One might call it language art through the very sounds. The word "play" gives more definition to pentecostal praxis and pathos than simply saying pentecostalism is experiential.

Experiential, yes, but a more refined definition is that it is the experience of play. Play, as noted by Vondey, is perhaps the best word to give language to pentecostal worship. This is not to say that play does not occur in other common grace experiences, but that it occurs often by accident and in spite of a more controlled entertainment purpose or performance.

The play moves worship liturgy beyond the purposes of propositional content being communicated in performance. Play for the sake of play (to borrow from "art for art's sake") denounces and empowers—the player cannot leave play unaltered. It creates space in any time, place, and people who step into it for re-visioning what is really real. Speaking in tongues is a kind of play that gives space for imagination leading to linguistic deconstruction, which opens up to prophetic imaginative speech. "Because God is an end in himself, he can liberate us from our purpose-oriented attitudes which destroy play."[39]

Quoting Romano Guardini, "the purpose of the liturgy consists of the fact that it is to be understood as the play of God's children before their God. The heart of the liturgy is not the extent of rationality but its capacity for a faithful and childlike imagination."[40] A more adult-sounding term that gets at this concept is *ecstasy*. In the baptism of the Spirit as understood by classical pentecostals, there is a "sense that one can transcend oneself in embracing God and the neighbor."[41] This is a transcendence that brings joy as well as empowerment and is a type of ecstasy. To wrap

39. Suurmond, *Word and Spirit*, 88.

40. Vondey, *Beyond Pentecostalism*, 131.

41. Macchia, *Justified*, 97.

back around in Christian language, this kind of speech enters into divine mystery, divine love as a non-mediated relationality. Faith grants access to receive this gift, but it is the work of the Spirit through the person that is "the abundant and excessive gift, faith is a weak vessel empowered by God."[42]

Relationality is part of the empowerment that occurs in play because it causes the person to enter into the flow of the power of the in-breaking, now-not-yet kingdom, the power of love. Put in other words, we enter the present and eschatological kingdom which is love, righteousness, peace, and joy in the Holy Spirit (Romans). Ecstasy is being caught up into another power and mode of being. In this case play of the Spirit in tongues helps one to be caught up into pathos and love that speaks to woundedness and to hope.

This place allows for the embrace across former walls of hostility and division and also creates an opening for a new community based on the coming reign of Christ. A clear manifestation of love in the open nature of this play is also a force to empower prophetic acting love in non-play life. One can see this demonstrated in both Acts 2:4–13, 42–47, 10:44–46, and 8:14–17. Cultural and religious biases are overcome—an act of forgiveness rooted in Christ, empowerment of persons, and liberation. The gift of "tongues speech" and then prophetic speech and acts precipitated this.[43]

This is present in pentecostal worship. "Tongues speech" empowers by helping all, even those most repressed by the rationally oriented worship in traditional power structures that formed old liturgies. Those "outside" can enter into their full personhood and restored power through speaking in tongues and the new space it creates in the inner person. There is no "doing it wrong" or out of sequence in the practice of "tongues speech" as prayer. Even when people are not literate or fluent in speech, they can raise their voices to heaven in the corporate prayer or worship gathering or alone while speaking in tongues. This finding of one's voice before being able to rearticulate in the language of the empire to those who may

42. Macchia, *Justified*, 55.

43. Macchia, *Justified*, 98.

be oppressors is also how we see "tongues speech" as empowering. Speaking in tongues is a form of play, and this play empowers.

1.3.1 The Problem of Disenchantment. Have We Relinquished the Wrong Things?

Relinquishment is crucial to the operation of the gifts of the Spirit, and layers of it occur in "tongues speech." As mentioned previously, a release of control over normal modes of speech is required in the mind of the person in order to choose to speak in tongues. Because it involves release of what is "proper," important, or expected, speaking in tongues is a language of marginality and liminality and stands even more so in contrast to the church or norms of empire. Seeking respectability can mean a capitulation of that which is "other" to that which is the norm of the empire. The genius of speaking in tongues is that it always pushes against imperial control, indeed against all control save for that of the one who can choose for themselves to seek and use the gift. Babylon does not choose "babble," rather babble comes upon its claims from the outside and exposes them as not being ultimate. Only One is ultimate, not the empire. "The Paraclete will bear witness against the world" is a Pneumatologic-Christology claim.[44]

"Tongues speech" is a negation of non-experiential truth claims. In this way it manifests the apophaticism of the Eastern Orthodox Church, which "teaches us to see above all a negative meaning in the dogmas of the church: it forbids us to follow natural ways of thought and to form concepts which would usurp the place of spiritual realities. For Christianity is not a philosophical school for speculating about abstract concepts, but is essentially a communion with the living God."[45] Pentecostals take on disenchantment of reductionism directly and most specifically in the speech practice of tongues. This charismatic gift "unites the material and spiritual dimensions of existence—the visible and invisible

44. Menzies, *Language of the Spirit*, 49.
45. Lossky, *Mystical Theology*, 42.

reality . . . the Spirit-baptized church becomes the embodied experience of heaven on earth—heaven transforming and transfiguring the earth into the Kingdom of God."[46]

Imagination is the seat of more than "false make-believe."[47] Yet much of Western Christianity seems to have lost or downplayed this experiential aspect of faith. When it comes to entering into the gifts of the Spirit, the recapturing of the imaginative and creative mind is important. Indeed it is through the "mind's eye" that these gifts are entered into. Worship is a re-imaging of the world through art and participation through material substance (action, creation, experience) in which we join the Spirit and word at play. Turning words into art experience is part of what is going on in the pentecostal use of language. Aesthetic philosophy is of help here to understand at least partly what occurs in speaking in tongues.

The liturgies of the Western church were influenced by the enlightenment. The use of Scripture as read through enlightenment tools reduced the Bible to being more transactional. The exchange of information through the pastor-teacher and also the liturgy had more pragmatic application focus for the community or individual. Over time this results in a church losing its ability to draw people into experiential encounter that forms at a deeper non-propositional level in worship.

Excursus: New Reformed Movement's Fundamental Incompatibility with Play

This brings us to a small excursus on the neo-reformed movement and its attempted co-option of the charismatic. The very nature of play require free actors, for when play is forced it is no longer play. It may retain some playfulness or simply devolve into entertainment for consumption, but it has lost the fundamental element of freedom.

46. Augustine, "Empowered Church," 174.
47. Boyd, *Seeing Is Believing*, 72.

The choice to enter the play of the Spirit and word as an individual is the ground from which play launches. A stroke against domination occurs when in spite of circumstance a person chooses to enter imaginative play. Play is a word and act against determinism of any kind. The generally deterministic Reformed worldviews inherently exclude genuine play. Even God cannot play with creatures if God is said to have exhaustively settled everything. God can use creatures to mimic play, but genuine play cannot exist in such a closed system.

It would be important to note that because play's nature is rooted in the very essence of the life of the Spirit, play is not without opposition. Internal resistance can be built up because of many personal or corporate "bad trip" common grace play experiences that were broken and twisted by sin and evil. The destruction of holy imagination or the diminishing of it is vital to the controlling and dominating work of Satan and those who have not awakened to the reality of dehumanizing spiritual warfare. We can rightly speak of non-play life as the primary sphere in which we live; however, this is not the same as an anti-play spirit. This is part of an anti-Christ destruction of a person's spirit that seeks suppression, guilt, or bondage to various religious or secular totalizing systems that maintain order by suppressing counter narratives. The counter-story against totalizing stories of control naturally arises in play of the common grace sort (art, sport, and the like) and certainly of the charismatic type as preeminently accessed in speaking in tongues. The play of tongues is a laugh at totalizing claims.

The problem of disenchantment and loss of faith is not new with Western civilization. The ancient Hebrews in exile had a similar issue. The Spirit of God, though, does not easily give ground to the world as given. The prophetic voice is a counter-story to what is assumed to be inherent in the world. So it should come as no surprise that any speaking the Holy Spirit does is at once a call to awaken and reenchant the human. The prophetic word in the common speech is one way this has been the case, but the "tongues speech" of the New Testament and all who have been willing to be unsettled in such speech find a reenchantment occurring. Speaking in tongues liberates the imagination to begin to dream anew by opening space in the mind, the imagination, of the tongues speaker. New sounds point to a new hope and the ecstatic language of another kingdom not bound by the rules of the old.

Disenchantment even to the point of loss of faith is a problem because it is the result of a flattened and controlled worldview. Someone's narrative and casting of what is "really real" has pushed out all other perspectives, not only ones that are lower on truth content, but also ones that call into question the powers as they are. This disenchantment has entered the worship and thinking of the church from time to time. The result is a church that is little more than the arm of the state or the powers that are, instead of the powers that are coming, forgetting the eschatological, forward-leaning vision of the church in worship. The negative work of the gifts of the Spirit in the church calls her to regain her posture in creation. With Lossky, we affirm that "the operation of the Holy Spirit in the world before the Church and outside the Church is not, therefore, the same as His presence in the Church after Pentecost."[48]

The power structures of the world work against the marginalized, or more accurately, they create marginalized peoples. These structures' fallen natures are sources of original disenchantment. One born into oppression, injustice, and the fallen structures of the world as given inherits a closed world. The oppressed and marginalized personally, by definition, never had an opening to power in the system. Their only access to original enchantment is through childhood play. Interestingly this is the same kind of belief that Jesus calls for in order for adults to be empowered and to overcome, as we will explore more.

"Tongues speech" is not direct prophetic speech in the usual sense (unless understood in interpretation as in Acts 2) as Paul makes clear in 1 Corinthians 14, but it does have a prophetic function to deconstruct or, to borrow from Jeremiah, to "tear down . . . [and] overthrow" and then re-vision what is real through imagination sustained in its play. This is also evidenced in Jeremiah's

---

48. Lossky, *Mystical Theology*, 157.

prophetic call, "to build and to plant."[49] This is one way in which I contend "tongues speech" names and calls out the powers by naming their lack of creativity and drive for control. Daniel Castelo, writing on the ecclesial holiness of the early pentecostal movement:

> The holiness that marks Pentecostal fellowship can never be reified or codified, for doing so would compromise a fruitful and innovative (i.e. Spirit-empowered and Spirit-led) future. When early Pentecostals practiced foot washing, advocated pacifism, allowed women to be ministers, and held services of diverse racial backgrounds, they did so not on the basis of maintaining a level of relevance by their observance of the status quo; quite the contrary, their apparent irrelevance to the conventions of their day was the bedrock of their alarming relevance, one that has become increasingly apparent to those of us who study the movement's history; they 'did not understand' what they were doing (cf. John 13:7), but at present we are coming to understand more and more the way the Spirit was leading this fellowship in the ways of holiness.[50]

Occasionally the "tongues speech" does get interpreted in the hearing of the congregation or the crowd, as in Acts 2. The initiatory Pentecost was indeed prophetic in direct and indirect ways. Speaking in tongues can be directly prophetic in that the tongues were understood by some in their languages; however, others considered even this initial xenolalia as "drunken babbling." Speaking in tongues is indirectly prophetic (not in understood language) by the visible testimony of *who* was filled with the Spirit and speaking in tongues. Peter interprets this prophetically following the initial speaking in tongues episode, through the lens of Joel's prophetic anticipation and also through Moses's prophetic anticipation (Num 11:30). "The community outburst of prophecy (Acts 2:1 referring to the 120 in v. 1:14), which fulfills Joel's oracle, had an earlier fulfillment in Luke's narrative when sons and daughters

---

49. "See, today I appoint you over nations and kingdoms to uproot and tear down, to destroy and overthrow, to build and to plant" (Jer 1:10, NIV).

50. Castelo, "Improvisational Quality," 103.

(John, Mary), the young and the old (John, Zacharias, Simeon, Anna and Elizabeth), and bond slaves (Mary, Simeon) became the prophetic precursors to Pentecost."[51] That all classes of people were now considered heirs to Moses's prophetic gift makes speaking in tongues prophetic in this way.

The immediate reconfiguring of language into non-propositional communication and verbal dance calls forth a picture of sound. It is also something that can only be silenced temporarily, but not ultimately controlled by the language-game power brokers of any culture or empire. Speaking in tongues sustains the ability of all who are open to it to enter into play at any time. There is nothing more to do other than to speak the tongues of prayer. Tongues calls us into play which exposes the technocratic approval: "The attitude of play . . . remains a zeal for truth and justice, even in times and situations in which this seems useless and crazy. So, people become living parables which can turn the world upside down and renew it."[52] I will argue later that speaking in tongues is a form of Spirit play which is perhaps the best at turning us into living parables.

There has been a decrease in speaking in tongues in North American Pentecostalism as more have sought to become, or have been co-opted by, middle-class, late-modern, American values such as individualism and consumerism. Menzies says, "Why would Pentecostals in the West, and especially in the U.S., move away from a doctrine and experience that have served us so well over the years? I believe that it is time to reconsider our willingness to embrace trendier, 'seeker-sensitive' approaches to church life that in many instances leave little room for speaking in tongues, especially in the corporate setting."[53]

Some have attributed this also to a desire for more union or identification with Evangelicalism from the 1940s onward.[54] One could argue that the current generation of Pentecostals has started

51. Stronstad, *Prophethood*, 65.

52. Suurmond, *Word and Spirit*, 90.

53. Menzies, *Speaking in Tongues*, 12; 7.

54. McQueen, *Joel and the Spirit*, 89.

to push back against that desire to be identified with Evangelicalism, at least Evangelicalism of the political variety. McQueen states, "The Spirit has been quenched [in North American Pentecostalism] through cultural, moral, institutional, and theological accommodation. The Spirit has become a domesticated helper who moves only within prescribed forms and at convenient occasion." He builds a case for lament in Joel as a doorway back into an eschatological focus of the Spirit again in North American Pentecostalism.[55]

The attempt to destroy play or bound it by the hegemon's rules also reveals another subversive aspect of the play of the Spirit. The Spirit will use any emotion and reaction-based emotion available to help God's people in time of need, suppression, and violence against them. The common grace art and the specific charism of speech can also empower in the face of direct hostility. We now explore this for a moment as we look at the power of lament.

1.4 Lament and Ecstasy as Related Experiences

The concept of lament as going beyond cognitive use of language to groans would also fit in this category of speech that includes tongues. Groans and communication without understandable words or cognitive content are also a form of Spirit-inspired, empire-avoiding speech. "In the same way, the Spirit helps us in our weakness, for we do not know how we should pray, but the Spirit himself intercedes for us with inexpressible groanings" (Rom 8:26, NET). Lament is also understood to be a gateway to personal and corporate liberation from the powers of sin and empire. Participating in a yearning for the judgment and justice of YHWH through acts of repentance and naming pain through non-cognitive language becomes a doorway to empowerment as well.[56]

Lament as part of repentance (turning) is part of the Christian journey of holiness. It is never finished in this life. Speaking

---

55. McQueen, *Joel and the Spirit*, 93.

56. McQueen, *Joel and the Spirit*, 33.

of this aspect of *theosis*, Lossky writes, "These charismatic tears, which are the consummation of repentance are at the same time the first-fruits of infinite joy: 'Blessed are ye that weep now: for ye shall laugh.' Tears purify our nature, for repentance is not merely *our* effort, *our* anguish, but is also the resplendent gift of the Holy Spirit, penetrating and transforming our hearts."[57]

For an adult the act of fully entering pain or an empathic reaction to others' pain becomes a type of play as well, because play is also accessed through pain. Letting pain surface through prayer can open one's emotions to be named, recognized, and reordered.

If one allows the body and mind to be joined in imagination with voice, deep groans are possible. This giving voice to pain can include non-propositional groaning which can open one to glossolalic speech. From groans to glossolalia, this movement brings about "emotional and intellectual integration."[58] In turn this movement empowers one in the journey. A key aspect we argue is that all Spirit-centered play produces a personal, and when in a group corporate, empowerment in the face of any and all circumstances.

Romans 8:26–27 has an outward intercessory or solidarity thrust which highlights God's ability to use tongues, with a free-will view of creation in mind, to work through human prayers that release spiritual power in circumstances the petitioner cannot personally know. This is mystical union for the benefit of creation and others, overcoming space and time limitations in a present or developing future situation.

When empire refuses even the right of words that name deep brokenness or injustice to be uttered, the power of groaning becomes apparent. "Above all people who go through the 'school of anxiety,' robbed as they are of civil and religious certainties (which function as idols), seem to be able to arrive at an experience of God."[59] Short of destruction of the individual, the groaning expresses the depth of injustice without providing prosecutable content for the unjust justice of the persecutor. Silence can also be

---

57. Lossky, *Mystical Theology*, 205.

58. McQueen, *Joel and the Spirit*, 107.

59. Suurmond, *Word and the Spirit*, 152.

part of protest. Silence demanded can be claimed by the oppressed and turned into silence as revolt against imperial speech. In this sense, "glossolalia and silence are functionally equivalent. . . . Both symbolize a response from the depths of the human spirit to the reality of God felt as immediate presence. . . . The difference may be as sub-dialects."[60]

The acts of groans, tears, lament, shouts, and "tongues speech" all function in bringing the participant into the arena of empowerment and liberation. This is a place of imagination, and when joined with the use of the whole being, another way to speak of it is play. The nature of the play is kinesthetic, causing an alignment of body and imagination which flows out of the charismatic accounts and gift uses in the New Testament and Hebrew Bible. We see this foreshadowed in the Spirit of YHWH coming upon the Hebrew prophets in dramatic speech and enactment. Speaking in tongues taps into, through play, future reality in the kingdom yet to fully come, the eschatological kingdom in the face of the broken kingdom of the world.[61]

What happens in the nature of Pentecostal liturgy is a ritualized "expression and de-structuralization"[62] of existing structures of power and values. The practice of "tongues speech" and the improvisation of the play of pentecostal worship have created spaces in Christianity that did not exist in most places. Even the old camp meetings without the "tongues speech" did not tear down the last barrier, which is always language. As Smith put it, "One might say such a prayer [glossolalic, speaking in tongues] in such a context [in a prayer response time at the close of a worship gathering] is a kind of sacramental practice of emptying, recognizing the failure of even language to measure up to such an exchange. Glossolalic prayer is an ongoing means, a sustaining means, of making oneself both receptive to and a conduit of the Spirit's work."[63]

60. Chan, *Pentecostal Theology*, 61.

61. Macchia, *Justified*, 51.

62. Vondey, *Beyond Pentecostalism*, 132.

63. Smith, *Thinking in Tongues*, 144.

"Tongues speech" is a model of crucifixion and resurrection. Just as water baptism is inspired as an imitation of death and resurrection, tongues is an ongoing representation of the fall and new life in one act. In this sense it is a sign of the new creation in Christ. Again, baptism signifies loss of the old, being buried with Christ and raised to newness of life with Christ. "Tongues speech" exposes the sin of power and disunity through the loss of language as a means to control and in the same stroke brings new language, new tongues, forth. Just as baptism requires a trusting relinquishment, so does speaking in tongues. The difference with speaking in tongues is that it can be entered into throughout life. It is a remembering of baptism in a very different way, a play that must be entered into to fully experience the empowering. The baptism of the Spirit results in this resurrection gift and play.

"Tongues speech" pushes the individual into a place of liminality. Between positions maintained by culture, society, and powers, this speech moves one into the place of becoming a living parable (albeit in short bursts or extended charismatic prayer). In entering "tongues speech," play is flipping expectations of what is considered normal life and normal paths of empowerment (e.g., control or ordering of life through language) and providing a direct empowering and liberating experience. In the groaning aspects of speaking in tongues there is an acknowledgement of deep brokenness, and yet the very speech imparts a sense of dignity and worth in the face of marginalization. This "dark play" experience is magnifying the voice of the oppressed, not allowing that voice to be "submerged in reality."[64] This direct empowerment comes through entering the realm of a spiritual kingdom, a kingdom of freedom, not defined by language, boundaries, material destruction. Speaking in tongues cracks up the "hegemonic certitude" of empire by empowering the prophetic voice.[65]

The empowerment comes as a mystical language that exposes the brokenness of our rituals. It is a kind of protest and iconoclasm against a one-sided, intellectually oriented faith approach.

64. Abraham, *Pentecostal Theology of Liberation*, 29, 33.

65. Brueggemann, *Practice of Prophetic Imagination*, 67.

Speaking in tongues is a type of truth-language, particularly in lament against evil. How does one give word to the deep brokenness of empire and its totalizing claims? It is the protest language which continually applies the ninth commandment against "utterance that distorts or misrepresents or skews."[66] Viable community that brings life for all depends on accurate, reliable utterance. When we are so far removed from the garden, how do we regain a sense of right speech? The Pentecostal can say that we do not; we receive it as a gift that denounces all our speech as a first prophetic move. This speech is against a world warped by false utterance and false power.

"Tongues speech" in the lament form points to the "not yet" and our hope rooted in the future. "Biblical eschatology, by contrast [with apocalypticism], links the present and the future by the Spirit as firstfruits of the new creation. It is as the firstfruits that we can begin to understand the Spirit's intercessory work in the church such as in Romans 8.26. The 'unutterable groanings' of the Spirit in the believers is not primarily concerned with our personal intimacy with God but the Spirit's work of identifying believers with the groanings of a broken world—a world that awaits the liberation of the children of God."[67]

1.5 Sustaining Reenchantment and Reawakening of the Imagination

Those who play will, moreover, constantly find their play thwarted by the dominant order, sometimes with fatal results.[68]

James Smith, in arguing that pentecostalism should see what is in creation as full of the Spirit, uses the term "enchanted naturalism" or "en-Spirited naturalism" or "noninterventionist supernaturalism."[69] The idea is that the Spirit is active in creation,

66. Brueggemann, *Word Militant*, 168.

67. Chan, *Pentecostal Theology*, 110.

68. Suurmond, *Word and Spirit*, 51.

69. Smith, *Thinking in Tongues*, 97.

not simply poking in here and there or not at all. In developing this third way, Smith states, "Instead pentecostal worship and practice are characterized by a kind of gritty materiality as space for work of the Spirit. Thus some pentecostal theologians have described pentecostal spirituality as *sacramental* in character."[70]

A Pentecostal worldview calls us to be reenchanted. One could argue that the highest language of enchantment is ecstatic speech, "tongues speech." Speaking in tongues bridges us from a natural–supernatural dichotomy to a merged, enmeshed view of the Spirit of God, the spirit of a person and the body. Indeed, it does not get any more "gritty" and enchanted than this. The reception of the language of tongues is gift not only *from* the Spirit, but also a living relationship *with* the Spirit, therefore spiritual and mystical. "Now it is the divine life which is opened up within us in the Holy Spirit. For He mysteriously identifies Himself with human persons whilst remaining incommunicable."[71] "Tongues speech" is one way this is most manifest.

In the Hebrew Bible part of the ministry of the prophets was reawakening imagination. Joel, which is central to giving an interpretive grid for the Day of Pentecost in Acts 2, speaks to this. In the Day of YHWH there is the enthronement of God over and against the powers of captivity. The promised messiah will sit on the throne and people will be given "new tongues" against the former speech of broken empire. The universal language of Acts is seen as part of that fulfillment after the ascension and enthronement of Christ in heavenly places.[72]

The loss of understanding the imagination as more than an internally bound faculty is confronted in the practice of "tongues speech." There is a reconfiguring and opening of the individual to sheer creativity and play. In order to understand how the strangeness or otherness of speaking in tongues works, we can look at the other ways in which people encounter the Spirit. Two ways of thinking about this are: (1) common grace experiences, and

---

70. Smith, *Thinking in Tongues*, 99.

71. Lossky, *Mystical Theology*, 172.

72. McQueen, *Joel and the Spirit*, 23.

(2) the unique (scandalous) grace encounters of the Spirit when Jesus is claimed and sought by a person and community (the charismatic).[73]

The first category is easily seen in the play of children, in sport, and in art. In common grace aesthetic experience, the Spirit engages with the person through play available in creation. We see this in our moments of being absorbed into play, whether art, sport, or simply delight in doing something or being somewhere. This also points to the non-dualistic, unified aspects of being that classical orthodox belief has always insisted on. These experiential encounters require body and spirit enmeshed. The material is needed for the encounter and empowers the spirit within. The spirit within helps the material aspect of embodiment to be awakened to its spiritual aspect, creating an empowering cycle.

"Tongues speech," as part of the charismatic particular experience, is acquired through a surrendering of certain kinds of control over thought and speech. One actively chooses to surrender and to leave open space in the mind for linguistic expression that is "babble," unknown or devoid of common meaning. This can be coupled with visualizing God's energies in various ways, wind or fire, for example. However, in and of itself there is a holy engagement in the mind and body of the one seeking this gift. It is gift because it is not an expected operation; it is gift because in first expression it is entirely unknown and new. This is something one does not grow into (in the initial encounter); words that are unknown must be spoken.

Imagination is letting go of making things conform to a certain reading of reality. This is often called "make believe," a strange phrase. Make, as in "force," belief in a nonreality is how we often use this phrase. However, when it comes to empowerment it is also about "making" as a creative engagement in which new belief about reality is formed. It is in this second aspect that holy imagination operates and brings about a new reality in the state of play, and this new reality comes out and touches non-play because it has altered something within the subject. Tongues, as such, is prophetic

73. Studebaker, *From Pentecost to the Triune God*, 250.

and a precursor to ongoing prophetic hope. "In an attempt to be relevant, churches have introduced the instrumental [utilitarian] thinking of the world and have thus become irrelevant."[74]

"Impossibility" is a word that is confronted and undone in "tongues speech" as well. "Tongues speech" helps craft through its very destructured nature new ideas of what is real and therefore reconnects one with a primal power of the Holy Spirit in creation. God uses this to remind and redefine what is possible in the speaker over against what is impossible and "commonly and reasonably accepted in the world."[75] This is part of the prophetic empowerment and imagination at work in each individual who welcomes and prays into the reality of this gift. Brueggemann states, "The first task of contemporary prophetic ministry is to empower and enable folk to *relinquish* a world that is passing from us."[76] In this way, speaking in tongues is most assuredly one gift well capable of assisting one in this right kind of relinquishment.

Bradley Truman Noel calls speaking in tongues and the openness to spiritual gifts an "experiential unification" which is the "Pentecostal edge." Pentecostals and charismatic churches that have surrendered their hermeneutics and experience-oriented theology and practices to a more common missional, evangelical approach lose something vital, and in fact needed, in the body of Christ, something needed for sustained mission, needed for an alternative mode of being Christian, and needed for prophetic voice grounded outside of a reaction against injustice. Speaking in tongues is part of sustaining a beatific and eschatological vision of Jesus, and the world, through the kingdom of God breaking in.

The freedom of God is on display in "tongues speech" as it is not controlled by language constructs of rationality.[77] This freedom runs in and through the mind of the one using the gift. The Holy Spirit then, through this gift, in turn uses the willing person to demonstrate the kingdom. The physical manifestation in

---

74. Suurmond, *Word and Spirit*, 95.

75. Brueggemann, *Practice of Prophetic Imagination*, 106.

76. Brueggemann, *Practice of Prophetic Imagination*, 136.

77. Brueggemann, *Practice of Prophetic Imagination*, 107.

speaking in tongues is not bound to the rules of the kingdom of this world and its hegemonic claims to correctly ordered speech. By deconstructing and reconstructing the role of speech in the play of speaking in tongues, rules that bind by limiting possibilities (pre-understanding) and which reduce imagination to "make believe" are flipped on their head. Speaking in tongues in particular makes the point that one can "know" things in a different way. This way is an embodied aesthetical way, a way of the Spirit. "This Pentecostal epistemology is a non-enlightenment enterprise, and places Pentecostal thought in a very different framework from conservative evangelicalism."[78]

---

78. Noel, *Pentecostal and Postmodern Hermeneutics*, 116–17.

CHAPTER 2

Liberation in Upside-Down Ways
The Way of Play and the Paraclete

2.1 Like Little Children

He called a child, had him stand among them, and said, "I tell you the truth, unless you turn around and become like little children, you will never enter the kingdom of heaven! Whoever then humbles himself like this little child is the greatest in the kingdom of heaven.

—MATTHEW 18:2–4 (NET)

The Holy Spirit is the true liberator. Pentecostalism is a major liberative force.[1]

For a child, the whole of life is a game. People who are not open to play cannot enter into the Kingdom of God.[2]

WE HAVE EXPLORED COMMON grace aspects of play, such as art and sport that empowers. We have spent some space regarding

1. Abraham, *Pentecostal Theology of Liberation*, 7, 25.
2. Suurmond, *Word and Spirit*, 48–49.

"tongues speech" as a charism that most consistently sustains a pathway for entering and experiencing Christ-centered, Spirit-empowered play. Jesus himself gives us another model to understand how to enter this Spirit empowerment through his teaching about children. Children easily blur the lines between play and non-play life. Play is a means of revealing to them how to live as future adults. The use of imagination, escape, and receiving gifts of sheer joy and identity is in the action of play.

The play of children is a gift of being and as such is a unmediated experience. Peter Althouse in his analysis of Suurmond relates, "Worship is 'useless' [non-utilitarian] because humans place themselves in the position of an unpretentious child who recognizes the gratuitousness of their existence and through worship enter into the noncoercive and vulnerable game of creation in their participation or play with Word and Spirit. Suurmond's proposal critiques modern atheist strategies that have infiltrated contemporary theology and liturgy as well as the pragmatic underpinnings that contribute to the secularization of Christianity in the West."[3] We have also mentioned earlier Smith's critique of naturalistic-reductionist worldviews' influence on the Western church. One should note that the ritual(s) which allow for play can be developed. The coercive reality we live in requires one to will to set aside time for ritual play, in choosing both to gather and then how the gathering actually function as enabling play. The play in worship, and speaking in tongues, itself is has a liberative force from all other aspects of life.

Children lost in play often lose their sense of secondary cultural boundaries. If allowed to play in a moderately safe place, gender, class, and ethnicity all fall away. Because play is a universal experience of children, walls are broken down between children in play and the play becomes the reality for that moment. Play is fundamentally something that teaches adults what is important and is also how we enter the kingdom of God. Our observation of and engagement with children is a path to our own liberation in adult community. The welcome of children in the church is not simply

---

3. Althouse, *Joel and the Spirit*, 276–77.

about passing on the faith to the next generation; when they are caught up in play in our community's midst it is a theological teaching directed at adults by Godself through these children. Children's play has a prophetic quality to it towards adults who claim to have a lock on reality. Most adults can point to moments in childhood when they remember being caught up in play. Children point us back to this reality and, as Jesus says, teach us that we must embrace the new realities created in play for our lives to mirror and enter the kingdom now and in the world to come.

It is speaking in tongues which most directly challenges our notions of adulthood and personhood. It challenges our command of intellect acquired through schooling and life experience. It undercuts our sense of needing to be rooted in that which we can order easily and calls us to revel in experience that is not under our cognitive control. We can step out of the play of tongues and analyze (as I am doing in this work); however, the play itself ultimately cannot be reduced down as much as the adult (Western) mind would prefer. There are those who choose to reject play in common grace and spiritual gift expression, but they do so by denying something central to the whole point of embodiment, which is to say they reject joy and the delight by being under the false idol of utility. Utility is important, but not our ultimate goal. We were created for work, yes, but work redeemed begins to move into a zone of play. We are created for play as well, and play can require work, particularly the work of moving beyond the control of anxiety and fear of death.

"Tongues speech" is perhaps the ultimate childlike experiential grace gift of the Spirit (charism). In contrast to all other gifts in the Scriptures, this one does not submit to utility. Its outflow certainly results in empowerment with liberation of the individual and charismatic community. However, the charism in operation is useless. It is this precise uselessness in expression that does the speaker the most good. It makes one childlike, vulnerable before self, God, and others. "Tongues speech" retains the charismatic playfulness of Jesus, his freedom. The life of Jesus threatened the order of the religious and political powers, and play does not submit easily to the interests of empire even when attempts are made to control it. Play still calls forth freedom in the secularly or religiously disempowered.[4]

"So whenever the [church] celebration is not sufficiently 'other,' the church lapses into activities which can be engaged in just as well or better by other groups."[5] There is a personal and social holiness that is informed and empowered by play, leading to different ways of being human in non-play life. Speaking in tongues sustains the "otherness" of the gathering of believers.

2.2 Play as Path to Theosis for Adults

The empowerment of the Spirit is also connected to the theosis work or divinization of the person by the work of the Spirit. We see this in liberation from a sin-shaped imagination and also in the sin-shaped kingdoms-of-the-world cultural divides. While on the one hand we can lean into our brokenness as Luther and Calvin restate Augustine's *simul justus et peccator* (just and a sinner at once), the other pentecostal hand says this is not adequate in light of the indwelling and baptizing ministries of the Spirit. "The Spirit—and not faith—is the abundant and excessive gift; faith is a weak vessel empowered by God."[6] To add the progressive dimension to Augustine's maxim, we can attach "in process" to the sinner part. This also shows the connection between Western ideas of progressive sanctification and Eastern Orthodox Church concepts of the ascent of the soul through practices of prayer. Speaking in tongues, when practiced regularly, can graciously empower the person in the way of becoming more like Christ. Gerd Theissen connects ecstatic speech of tongues with a love experience with God pouring out the Spirit into our hearts to "reshape those sins

---

4. Suurmond, *Word and Spirit*, 129.

5. Suurmond, *Word and Spirit*, 95.

6. Macchia, *Justified*, 46, 55.

and habits of which we may be unaware. Sin and sanctification are not just conscious matters."[7]

The use of speaking in tongues helps form an alternative picture of oneself which leads forward in the process of personal liberation from the internal "givens." Speaking in tongues gives shape and space as a type of play. This leads to affective movement, forming new emotions. As such, it is also creative in expanding human nature beyond original limits as a result of formation up to this point in one's life and cognitive assumptions. Put another way, "affective transformation occurs being caught up in a larger narrative—a new story."[8] This is empowerment for holy living through a new vision of being human, shaped by the teachings of Jesus, imagined in the language of the Spirit in the mind, body, and voice of the one who uses the gift. To be clear, although speaking in tongues is an aspect of empowering holy choice in the believer, it is still very much relational. Even speaking in tongues can exist in a person who does it perfunctorily instead of with a growing yieldedness in imagination as they practice the gift. The continued practice of the gift, though, will still shape and reshape the imagination. In this way it empowers a life of repentance.

Luke-Acts relays that the power which Jesus acted on was also promised by him and God the Father: "But you will receive power when the Holy Spirit comes on you; and you will be my witnesses" (Acts 1:8). There is also the promise of assistance, comfort, and guidance to be provided directly by the Holy Spirit as relayed in John's Gospel, 14:26. In face of persecution, which is imperial in nature, there is a promise of empowerment.[9]

The play that produces new imagination has personal import in holiness through seeing self and life differently than cultural and natural givens. It also, of course, has a social component. The individual, when reimagining self, cannot help but also reimagine circumstances, both immediate and those present in global society. Often this universal awakening will lead to overwhelmed emotions.

7. Thiselton, *Holy Spirit*, 120.

8. Coulter, "Whole Gospel," 160.

9. Menzies, *Language of the Spirit*, 49.

This, in turn, leads the person back into play in order to process and to cope. Such a person has been fundamentally awakened to the larger picture of brokenness and beauty in the created world. "Tongues speech" opens the imagination and produces prophetic vision with words. The group experience of speaking in tongues can itself be unifying across former divides. Speaking of the Los Angeles Azusa Street Revival, Suurmond reflects that William Seymour was said to have viewed "glossolalia above all as the sign that Spirit was breaking through the barriers between races, sexes, and nationalities and was reconciling all people with one another. . . . He saw this confirmed when blacks and whites, Americans and foreigners, professors and washerwomen prayed and sang together with sounds of glossolalia. In this way people who have no common language experienced a unity which transcended the barriers of language."[10] Prophetic utterance moves power from the kingdoms of the world and circumstance and reassigns it to God.[11] Speaking in tongues empowers action in the face of the brokenness through words that move and reassign power, leading a drive towards social holiness. This would also reflect Wesley's teaching that there is no personal holiness without relationship; holiness is always relational, or social, in nature.[12]

The later bifurcation of holiness into private and public realms gave rise to the use of social holiness as a prophetic justice issue. "Tongues speech" empowers the individual to reclaim more fully their personhood and to be known as a valuable part of society. The Spirit drives the person toward relationship in the church (community of believers) and also toward action in the kingdom of the world as part of the society of the church. Speaking in tongues transforms persons into a community of prophets. The act of praying in tongues in a church setting is communal empowering of prophetic being in which the walls of male/female, rich/poor, and Jew/Greek are broken down. When the play of the Spirit, guided by the word, takes place in community, a play is unleashed

10. Suurmond, *Word and Spirit*, 6.

11. Brueggemann, *Practice of Prophetic Imagination*, 30.

12. Watson, "Wesley Didn't Say It."

that is a foretaste of the kingdom of God. It also reveals that this gift moves beyond a private blessing to a community empowered, a community of prophets.[13] Chan speaks to this regarding the Pentecostal event: "Speaking in tongues . . . is the most appropriate symbol of an event whose primary purpose was to create a church distinguished chiefly by its all-embracing inclusiveness." Tongues is a language which points to a universal experience by swapping out the normal function of language and performs by providing a type of social holiness.[14]

2.3 Gift and Play

Gifts of healing and exorcism provide some obvious works of physical liberation.[15] I argue that speech gifts also do this at a more holistic level. However the Spirit manifests, s/he "will bear witness against the world."[16] "Tongues speech" is first and foremost a gift. Gifts received by children, who have not yet learned to over-analyze the nature of gift, are helpful, indeed "biblical," in understanding the doorways into this reenchanted world. Spiritual gifts, like speaking in tongues, may seem excessive or gratuitous, but "a true gift defies a comparable gesture. . . . Humans never give true gifts."[17] We are, however, called to grow in our capacity to give true gifts, leading towards a fully holy humanity, a full restoration of the image and likeness of God.

Gifts are anticipated with joy, and good gifts are received with joy by children. The very seeking of a gift or anticipation of a gift is a source of joy. This is one reason why Pentecostal worship easily enters into the realm of the joy of God. The very nature of gift creates a new emotional state. Spiritual gifts challenge the status quo simply by teaching and learning of their possibility. This, the

---

13. Abraham, *Pentecostal Liberation*, 74, 77, 85.

14. Chan, *Pentecostal Theology*, 103.

15. Abraham, *Pentecostal Liberation*, 37.

16. Menzies, *Language of the Spirit*, 49.

17. Macchia, *Justified*, 167.

expectation that God, your Heavenly Father, will give *good* gifts, is another area in which we are commanded to be like children.

The play of the Holy Spirit begins in a body of believers and seekers when they learn that gifts are involved. We see this in Acts 13:52—when the Holy Spirit moved after the gospel was shared and the disciples were persecuted, they were given as a gift a "filling with joy." Gifts such as speaking in tongues bring out clearly the experience of play and joy. "Glossolalia is the charism which is more similar to laughter. It is spontaneous, useless (because it consists of meaningless sounds), and is experienced as broadening and healing."[18]

Gifts carry with them the unknown and often the unnecessary, at least unnecessary in our perception. The sacraments are visible gifts as well. Speaking in tongues fits within this category as a sacrament in Pentecostalism. Menzies writes, "I find it interesting that so many believers from traditional churches today react negatively to the notion of glossolalia as a visible sign. They often ask, should we really emphasize a visible sign like tongues? Yet these same Christians participate in a liturgical form of worship that is filled with sacraments and imagery; a form of worship that emphasizes visible signs. Signs are valuable when they point to something significant. Luke and his church clearly understood this."[19] Pentecostal worship, and "tongues speech" in general, creates space for "a certain aimless playfulness." Moreover, speaking in tongues incarnates a spiritual reality that "God graces the gibberish."[20] The very concept of gift requires a giver and a receiver, so it is intimately connected with relationship. While I argue against a reductionist utilitarian view of play and gift, there is a sense in which a gift does feed a relationship. In the case of God there is no requirement of reciprocity, but rather a loving ask. It would seem God delights most in "the ask" from the person and in giving a gift does not demand that one use or play with it.

---

18. Suurmond, *Word and Spirit*, 79.

19. Menzies, *Speaking in Tongues*, 38.

20. Chan, *Pentecostal Theology*, 79–80.

A digression into a relational theology of love is required as well. Love of the highest order is experienced in play. In play we experience the love of the players through presence and interaction. Playing with a child expresses to them the gift of love through time, in loss of all other priorities for that moment of play, and this love in turn makes all other aspects of life together renewed, with the *telos* being love. Play sustains love; love holds up the universe. Love as sheer gift is built in us as we learn to enter play with others. In this sense we could say there is some utility in play in sustaining and experiencing the freest love. Speaking in tongues does, however, reduce any other utility in the actual play of the speech.

Worship in the pentecostal church is about expressing love through the play of body, Scripture, art, word, and the ministry of praying for and naming the needs and concerns of one another. Celebration is a good word to use to speak of most of what occurs in an open liturgy, such as is traditionally the case in Pentecostal/Charismatic worship. Tongues is a central part of this. Interpreting Paul, Menzies indicates that speaking in tongues is "doxological prayer.... [He connects] speaking in tongues and joyful prayer and thanksgiving."[21] The celebration forms and shapes the players. It is the fashioning of and empowering of love that brings about true holiness, and the creature is made whole in the celebration. "The Spirit, in Trinity, opens the Godhead beyond I–Thous, to include the many." The Holy Spirit is "Person-love. He is Person-Gift."[22]

Worship in the Anabaptist or Pentecostal church is (or should be) a liturgy that creates space for gifts of the Spirit to be manifest in the gathered face–to–face community. That is to say, we need to create planned environments for the body to speak, sing, reflect, and respond to the word and Spirit. We should use ancient and modern resources to craft a weekly gathering for this to happen. These things, which allow for the planned spontaneity of play and intentionally invite others into it, create the atmosphere for love to be experienced by the players. Relationship is "a more basic category for understanding the nature of the world of the Spirit

21. Menzies, *Speaking in Tongues*, 137.
22. Macchia, *Justified*, 302–3.

than mission," Chan states rightly, even beyond mission.[23] Mission flows out of empowered love.

The Lukan telling of Jesus' teachings on the Father giving good gifts and also the reception of the kingdom as a child are important. "Glossolalia, in a unique way, symbolizes this challenge [for the church to be on apostolic mission and growing from charismatic roots]. It reminds us of our calling and our need of divine enabling."[24] Here Luke (who focuses less on justification by the Spirit than Paul does, but on the Spirit as the relationally given, empowering agent of the mission of God) is important for our argument of empowerment of the unempowered.

The relationship of God the Father/Mother, the Son, and the Spirit given through this interwoven relationship to people should clue us in to the importance of the Spirit's work as rooted in God's love for us and for all. This is an overwhelming experience and as such the main lover gives more than the receiver can possibly understand. A mystical encounter, a theophany, occurs in the gift of the Spirit and the overflow results in "tongues speech." Again we turn to Chan, who states, "The revelation of God, the primal reality, results in a human response in primordial words which are their own explanation for that theophany. . . . The physical act of speaking in tongues is not only a pointer to but also embodies the spiritual reality: 'the primordial word is in the proper sense the presentation of the thing itself.' . . . The whole experience is characterized by an active passivity."[25]

Children are for us a model of liberation. The nature of a child's place in the ancient world is important to note. They were in no way considered powerful nor placed in a seat of priority as children of the privileged Western world tend to be. Young children play, and often this play prepares them for "real" world life. We make a big mistake in thinking we do not need to play as adults in order to make a different kind of difference in the non-play "real" world. "Tongues speech" dethrones our idolatry of language and

---

23. Chan, *Pentecostal Theology*, 45.

24. Menzies, *Speaking in Tongues*, 40.

25. Chan, *Pentecostal Theology*, 51.

self-importance. The practice tells us that preparation and change in the "real" occurs first in the unreality of holy imagination producing social and personal liberation.

"Holiness" is the classical term Pentecostals use to speak of liberation from things that control and suppress us personally and socially. Speaking in tongues, glossolalia, "symbolizes new possibilities of social and political relationships."[26] Engaging in speaking in tongues as holy play denounces the "stop playing!" command of what is declared by the powers of bondage to be "normal." In speaking in tongues, "normal" is overturned to make room for new and more vibrant ways of being.

Language is always a means used to order and control the world and often other people. It is also fallen and will not be fully redeemed until the new creation, where "tongues speech" will no longer be necessary as a gift. It is no mistake that "tongues speech" attacks the root of our idolatries of control and manipulation which are always manifested through language. There is a holiness of language that only occurs in the magical language of "tongues speech," because only empowerment can come forth from it, and no abuse of the subtle but more powerful idolatry of language games. It's the parable that cannot be domesticated in the second hearing.

An aspect of liberation with tongues is the way it opens communication and relationship through prayer between those who do not share any human language. Gifts of the Spirit open imaginative mission through a strange type of radical hospitality.[27]

2.4 Speaking in Tongues as Liberation-Sustaining Speech

The non-captive parabolic nature of tongues enables it to continue its liberative function cross-generationally. This is the fundamental problem of the classic parable, its domestication. Speaking in

---

26. Mittelstadt, *Reading Luke-Acts*, 119.

27. Mittelstadt, *Reading Luke-Acts*, 135.

tongues resists this; it can only be re-marginalized as has happened in many Pentecostal churches after their liberative lift in North America and Europe. The divine genius of tongues is its built-in resistance to control. It can only be silenced, and even then one can pray in the mind.

Tongues can also be understood as empowering because it has the capacity to be community sustaining. Many have experienced a social and economic uplift through tongues, but then give away the strangeness of tongues in order to be seen as part of normal society or evangelical subgroups. This desire to fit in is a temptation that has a cost, and that cost is the loss of the Spirit's gift of decentering "tongues speech." Long-term results are the decrease in prophetic push back, eschatological hope, and ability to identify with those on the margins. To the degree that Pentecostals in North America turn from "tongues speech," they lose the power of creating new community and social reordering. They lose the power of liberation inherent in speaking in tongues. "The justice of the Spirit is *koinoia* or a sharing of life."[28] To reject this new community for old community and its demands is to submit oneself back into a type of slavery.

Play of the Spirit creates a new community of the players. "The Spirit is present in the church in a way . . . that he is not present in the world."[29] Speaking in tongues is also a universal language, not in its ability to communicate propositionally, but in its ability to unify the speakers in their theophanic corporate experience. Unity is sustained in tongues also because "tongues speech" leans in to universal justice and eschatological hope. It is the language of a kingdom yet to come fully. Justice requires the undoing of the whole world and a simultaneous speaking forth of a new world. "The justice of [Spirit-created] *koinonia* is not assimilation to a controlling group ego but a communion of diverse voices, all of which are uniquely loyal to God's justice in the world."[30] Tongues

28. Macchia, *Justified*, 274.

29. Chan, *Pentecostal Theology*, 110.

30. Macchia, *Justified*, 110.

is a universal language rooted in an experience to come. "The re-making of language symbolizes the remaking of history."[31]

2.5 Sustaining Parable with the Play of Tongues— Turning People into Walking Parablers

Child's play and noncommunicative language practices continu-ally produce empowerment and challenge new norms. This is like hearing a parable. The nature of parable is that in the first hearing, the speech and act remain largely in control of the one spinning forth the parable, the "parabler" (to use Crossan's term). "Parable is set in this world but is not of this world and precisely because of that, it is in a position to change it. Like an icebreaker, a parable makes a gap in our closed order and thus creates room for God's rule."[32] In teaching, Jesus frequently used the parable as a literary device in which common understanding of life and story is sub-verted to reveal and bring the hearers into a new understanding. Crossan argues that "myth establishes world. Apologue defends world. Action investigates world. Satire attacks world. Parable subverts world. . . . It is possible to live in myth and without par-able. But it is not possible to live in parable alone. . . . [Parable] is a story deliberately calculated to show the limitations of myth, to shatter world so that its relativity becomes apparent."[33] It is my contention that "tongues speech" is a spiritual gift of aesthetic em-bodiment and, in particular, is a linguistic art making a parable of all language. This further defines how speaking in tongues is a preprophetic prophetic empowerment and unmediated liberation experience.

Speaking in tongues does something a parable as conven-tionally understood cannot do after the initial telling. A parable loses its initial punch in the retelling because the initial impact has had time to be domesticated the more times one hears a parable.

---

31. Chan, *Pentecostal Theology*, 53.

32. Suurmond, *Word and Spirit*, 51.

33. Crossan, *Dark Interval*, 42.

When it is told across time and culture, the punch, which would have been clear to the initial audience, has to be explained in the interpretive and translated telling, providing the context and detail along with the related emotional experiences. So the subversive value is filtered and decreased significantly from the impact the original performative aspect of the play of parable would have had on an audience.

Parable was one of Jesus', God-in-the-flesh's, favored ways to bring about spiritual awakening and synergistic cooperation of those he taught. Interestingly, this speech-act was not duplicated by the apostles. We maintain that this is rooted in two reasons. First, that the early church was fully aware they were becoming a living parable against the narrative claims and the language of control of the Roman Empire and Second Temple Judaism. Second, that the power of table-flipping, paradigm-challenging prophetic speech was embedded in their Spirit-inspired speech—not only through prophetic delivery of the *Kyrgema*, but (more to the point of this work) most dramatically in ongoing "tongues speech." Third, they were still in close temporal proximity to Jesus' life; the later church would rediscover the use of story and parable.

"Tongues speech" maintains the disruptive nature of parable by attacking the very means of control, the cognitive use of language for the hearer, and historical domestication. To borrow from Crossan again, "Parabolic religion [is] a religion that continually and deliberately subverts final words about 'reality' and thereby introduces the possibility of transcendence."[34] As a form of prophetic speech, speaking in tongues stands "outside the 'official' cult speech, resulting in 'extreme boldness' as newly minted speech."[35] The net is not simply a non-cognitive communication babble; it results in empowerment for those who choose to go beyond critique or analysis and engage in it. So one function of "tongues speech" is turning the person into a living parable, a localized theophany who experiences the immanent and transcendent at once as s/he or the group speaks in tongues. The biblical texts that point to

34. Crossan, *Dark Interval*, 105.

35. Abraham, *Pentecostal Liberation*, 53.

"tongues speech" and then to the cognitively clear, yet Spirit-inspired, prophecy or other language (charismatic) gifts as the initial evidence of Spirit-baptism in Luke-Acts are telling. Our words must be altered and in new relationship with the Spirit in order to affect kingdom outcomes in the current situation. The outflow is a new power for mission in the face of overwhelming odds in the favor of other culturally compelling myths that give competing final words about reality.

It is also important to note that the cognitive use of language is how the mission is engaged. "Tongues speech" is not the local language of mission, it is the universal mystical prophetic language of empowerment and *sustaining* mission. It empowers mission and liberates the one who prays in tongues. It is (as explored elsewhere in this thesis) play that must then be left to enter into non-play, or more naturally-supernatural aspects of Christian existence. To use Crossan's language, one cannot live in parable. Menzies makes a lesser claim than I am here regarding speaking in tongues and parable: "Our experience of glossolalia, like the 'tongues speech' of Acts 2, represents an enacted parable that reminds us of our true calling and ultimate destiny."[36] I believe that speaking in tongues does that and much more in terms of parable.

Walter Brueggemann argues that counter-narrative is essential kingdom of God speech.[37] This comes, for exiles, from the preaching of prophetic texts. Pentecostal "tongues speech," however, can precede and preempt prophetic preaching when the preaching is not taking place or when those in control of the telling are still more aligned with empire than kingdom. Speaking in tongues also confronts the problem of history being written by the winners; the act of speaking in tongues itself can be faked, but it is not something which can be directly related and retold, it has to be entered into as an experience by each person. It is the speech of play and that of a holy fool, and cannot be a mediated experience. It is a mystical experience with a buil-in protection from control of the speech and its work in the person's body and mind.

36. Menzies, *Speaking in Tongues*, 161.
37. Brueggemann, *Word Militant*, 56.

In light of the normal, non-play aspects of life, speaking in tongues is a kind of insanity. To quote Abraham, "Prophets lived in a kind of insanity. . . . [They exercised] freedom to differ, the courage to condemn, and folly to hope."[38] The prophets in the Hebrew Bible had the ancestral narratives of Israel to work with. These "ancestral narratives attest to the power of YHWH to create new historical possibilities where there is no ground for expectation." However, to enable the prophetic empowerment to all, even those who are locked out of accessing those narratives, requires granting the living Spirit behind those narratives to the many. "Tongues speech" does that by providing the words beyond cognition, bringing the power behind, in, and through to bear. It also then enables one to see oneself back in to the history of Israel. This is the Spirit that empowered Moses and the seventy-two, the prophets, Jesus, and the early church, and still empowers people today.[39]

Language is a method of primary communication. It is also a way we try to control our world. This can be both good and bad. All governments, and indeed entire industries, use language as a means of exerting control, order, spin, and often perpetuating injustice. Of course the educated and articulate can often find ways to push back against this use of language. However, in places where people have been so crushed that their access to the power of language to change the narrative is limited, more empowered people who have been awakened or convicted can join them and "share" some of their "say-so"—this is standing in solidarity with oppressed people. (We should not confuse the truly oppressed with people who merely *say* they are oppressed. While they certainly may have a case, if their message is getting out they are the "semi-privileged oppressed.")

We often use gifts as a way to empower others in the Western world, but there is an expectation that the liberation through the solidarity of gifting will result in people who also affirm our cultural values. God, however, has not bought into our Western values of emotion and culture (although many are shaped by things

38. Abraham, *Pentecostal Liberation*, 55–6.

39. Brueggemann, *Practice of Prophetic Imagination*, 11.

that *do* align with Jesus' life and teaching, many are anti-kingdom as well). "Tongues speech" declares all have something to say locally after its empowerment, but, strangely, "tongues speech" also declares a powerful universal Christian humanism by showing that all have words of mystical power to speak. "Many Pentecostals discovered for the first time in Charismatic celebration that they have something to say. . . . They do this in the play of the Charismatic celebration but also in glossolalia, in which they give expression to what [certainly with a limited command of language] can never be expressed adequately, the love of God in Christ. In a sense Glossolalia is the democratic counterpart of a talent for poetry."[40]

Gifts of the Spirit, in particular those that go straight to the Western hegemony of language, are greatly needed for the Western church to pivot into a new posture of power-under in a post-Christendom world. Tongues helps us enter the "as if" eschatological true worship of God. Melissa Archer says, "False worship, such as John portrays in the worship of the beast, is false precisely because its object is not the transcendent mystery, but only the mystification of something finite." [41]

"Tongues speech" and prophetic speech are God-given means of making such a pivot from a palace mindset to being on the margins. Brueggemann indicates that root sins and targets of prophetic critique are self-invention and self-suffering. Archer, writing on Pentecostal worship as being shaped by eschatology, states, "It is by engaging in the liturgy of heaven that John's hearers are to counter the false liturgies around them."[42] Speaking in tongues is referred to as praying in the Spirit and as heavenly tongues because it brings union with worship beyond the domain of settled speech. In deconstructing our normal use of language and the empowerment over and against the norms of language, speaking in tongues is well suited.[43] "Tongues speech" in particular hits the pride of control through one's language head-on. Moreover, we are finding

40. Suurmond, *Word and Spirit*, 155.

41. Archer, *'I Was in the Spirit,'* 311.

42. Archer, *'I Was in the Spirit,'* 311.

43. Brueggemann, *Practice of Prophetic Imagination*, 4.

the explosion of Christianity around the globe in places where people are open to this who have usually been oppressed. Apparently there is some direct empowerment that occurs that changes the course of life for people, an empowerment that jumps over the idolatry of language as a means of control or domination. It begins with direct, divine, sheer gift that is somewhat unexplainable and then moves into alternative-city (e.g., churches) empowerment. To quote Robert Menzies, "It is a risky thing to encounter God. Speaking in tongues symbolizes this risk, for it requires that we surrender control of that most significant and defining organ of our body, our tongue (Jas 3:1–12, Prov 18:21)."[44] Again, "tongues speech" is a gift that you can experience, but its non-communicative yet empowering effect is a gift that you can have but not "know" in a control sort of way. It is a brilliant stroke to constantly bring the tower of Babel down across powers, thrones, ages, cultures; the kind of crazy artist stroke that keeps painting across time. It is the order of God over the control impulses of men and women, regardless of whether they are religious or secular in nature. Tongues turn people into a community of living parablers, prophets who are not captive to an earthly kingdom.[45]

Speaking in tongues is a disturbing gift. It disturbs the speaker and the hegemon. The marginalized are disturbed and become agents of disruption through "tongues speech," which sustains turning and disruption as it turns into culture-transformation and then back into new (prophetic) speech against the powers of domination. The Spirit-driven liberationist aspects of speaking in tongues have a built-in oppression-checking aspect. The tongues remain uncontrollable by the powers, enabling psychological pushback for the one expressing this gift. "The fact that so many liberation movements in history that were confidently hailed as signs of the Spirit turned out later to be just as oppressive and constrictive as the systems they replaced shows that discerning the Spirit in the world is not as easy as it is often made out to be. . . . What we would like to believe is the sign of God's Spirit often

44. Menzies, *Speaking in Tongues*, 7.
45. Stronstad, *Prophethood*, 80.

betrays a preference of one human ideology over another."[46] Hence to speak in tongues is to constantly critique all ideologies at their foundation—the continual idolatry of language itself.

We should add that capital "P" pentecostals (not all, but the spectrum in classical "P" groups tend to abuse or ignore "tongues speech") often miss the boat by a mile on "tongues speech" because they seek to domesticate and control it, or ignore it and whitewash it. The "giftedness" of speaking in tongues can be lost in how the traditioning is done in classical Pentecostal circles. There should be a healthy emphasis on being open and pursuing various pathways into receiving this gift, but it can quickly become toxic when "forced" by insisting it is *the* Initial Physical Evidence for an individual. That is beyond the scope of this paper, but other gifts, which are subjectively and objectively received after or during a prayer for an infilling of the Spirit (one which goes beyond the baptism of the Spirit by the church and indwelling of the Spirit at conversion), may certainly precede one's seeking and reception of the gift of speaking in tongues. There are other "evidential" speech gifts. What Acts makes clear is that inspired "speech" gifts are multilayered initial physical evidences. So the gift of primal empowerment and play becomes a shadow, or at worse a knockoff, if it is forced to the front of the line for everyone. Instead of seeking and eventually receiving speaking in tongues with joy and entering into play, it (the seeking process) can devolve into another form of human control and division.

Instructive as well are the common grace parallels to spiritual-gift-centered play. Everyone is called into play easily when they are children. Hence Jesus talks about becoming childlike in receiving the kingdom. This is directly connected to the Holy Spirit's work now, and of course part of that work is the giving of spiritual gifts. As adults we have to be more intentional about making space and time for play, whether through nature, game, sport, or art—however we find it easiest to enter into that state of play or creative flow. Being forced into the game causes one to resist entering the experience of play, or to simply desire to get it over with already.

46. Chan, *Pentecostal Theology*, 112.

The other significant piece here is what happens in this kind of speech. The parallels for everyone occur in (common grace and experience) play (as defined in the preceding paragraph); you are taken up out of "normal" or non-play life into play; you experience fun, joy, and intensity and are empowered outside of whatever else and other powers there are in order to enter back into your non-play life differently. In Jesus and the sending of the Holy Spirit (and in the ongoing filling and sending in the Lukan sense) you are invited to be empowered at the deepest level of being. So charismatics, pentecostals, and Pentecostals need to do a better job of communicating about this "non-communicative" empowerment. They should teach and invite, with gracious, humble hospitality, more people into the play of the Spirit without downplaying or devaluing it. It is a huge mistake to do so, to surrender the "furniture in the room" of theological discourse to those who are too captive to enlightenment or late-modern thinking regarding the nature of being and experience.

CHAPTER 3

Cultivating Tongues Speech and Holy Imagination

I wish you all spoke in tongues.

—1 Corinthians 14:5

In this chapter I seek to detail ways to teach about and cultivate the gift speaking in tongues. These are, of course, tentative handles that may be of help in a preaching- or more study-praxis-oriented church. Walter Hollenweger states, "The function of the Pentecostal movement is to restore the power of expression to the people without identity and powers of speech, and to heal them from the terror of the loss of speech."[1] Paul is quite clear that in the gifts of the Spirit we have a cooperant role to play. "With regard to spiritual gifts, brothers and sisters, I do not want you to be uninformed." And again in chapter 14, "Pursue love and be eager for the spiritual gifts."[2] All of the following suggestions are based on a church that understands that the play of the worship gathering is intended to maximize participation in an orderly way, a way which also requires a mental and planning shift from liturgy and worship

1. Suurmond, *Word and Spirit*, 62.
2. 1 Cor 12:1, "uninformed," or in the Greek "ignorant." 1 Cor 14:1.

as "performance for," or even worse "entertainment of," the gathered community of believers and seekers. "In particular, the root metaphor of 'performance' privileges usefulness, purposefulness, productivity, and orderliness [control?] over human existence. It gives priority to cognition without an adequate representation of other elements of human life."[3] Speaking in tongues in this sense is anti-performance.

It should be obvious that any church which desires people to experience and operate in liberation would want a gift in operation which is about breaking free from hegemony. If the good news is to be truly good, it has to change the person and the control that seeks to and succeeds in oppressing and dominating them. Turning all people into prophets through the gift of tongues means they can become "charismatic centers of power" and an empowered charismatic community of prophets.[4] As Menzies points out, in 1 Corinthians 12 Paul is only limiting the use of tongues in the public assembly to some, while encouraging all people to speak in tongues in the personal or prayer context in order to take the elitist claim about tongues away from the few who seem to think it's not available to everyone, and therefore are misusing and lording the gift over others. "In other words, when Paul asks, 'Do all speak in tongues?' he is not asking, 'Can all speak in tongues (in private or corporate contexts)?' Rather, he is making a point very much in line with what precedes in chapter 12: when we gather together, not everyone contributes to the body in the same way; not everyone speaks in tongues or interprets in the corporate setting, do they?"[5]

3.1 Affirm Foolish Joy "Aimless Playfulness"

And do not get drunk with wine, which is debauchery, but be filled by the Spirit, speaking to one another in psalms, hymns, and spiritual

---

3. Althouse, *Joel and the Spirit*, 277.

4. Abraham, *Pentecostal Liberation*, 60.

5. Menzies, *Speaking in Tongues*, 93.

songs, singing and making music in your hearts to the Lord, always
giving thanks to God the Father for each other.

—EPHESIANS 5:18–20A (NET)

As we have explored earlier in play, there is a multilayered experience of joy that occurs in gift-giving and in play. The gifts of the Spirit are eschatological and prophetic signs of a kingdom of joy.[6] Because they reach beyond the known of any circumstance as seen by the naturalistic, enslaved mind, it is surprising to people when such a gift is expressed. It is the breaking of this reductionist slavery that also opens the way for joy as a gift. Playing through speaking in tongues in particular can give voice to joy as a sheer gift as a result of a quick breaking of a former mindset. "These foolish (Charismatic) expressions help to break through the excessive control of the analytical intellect and to make us open to an encounter with God in the deeper levels of our being."[7] "Play rather than performance is a better metaphor . . . it invites all to participate fully rather than to sit passively under the performance of a professional."[8]

Paul and Silas in prison exhibit this joy in their knowledge of a great kingdom at hand. Chan notes that there is "a certain aimless playfulness is the Pentecostal way of life, especially in worship."[9] It would need to be said that the face-to-face gathering of the church is vital to provide the location and context of entering into the experience of the Spirit and also the context for hearing, seeking, and expressing the gift of tongues. "The play of the Spirit and Word is crucial for structuring Pentecostal spirituality. But this play cannot be carried out effectively if it is not satisfactorily located in ecclesiology. For play to continue, there must be a playground where the rules of the game are clearly established, that is, a stable traditioning structure."[10]

6. Abraham, *Pentecostal Liberation*, 37.

7. Suurmond, *Word and Spirit*, 79.

8. Althouse, *Joel and the Spirit*, 277.

9. Chan, *Pentecostal Theology*, 79–80.

10. Chan, *Pentecostal Theology*, 100.

Suurmond makes the point that "the crown of creation is not human beings[!], who were created on the sixth day, but the Sabbath, made on the seventh and last day of creation. . . . Sabbath tells us 'the world is destined for the messianic time: oriented on being with God in complete freedom and delight." For a whole day we remember it is grace, not work, that saves us. One significance of worship gatherings is the enjoyment of creation and the delight of entering in to play. Worship is childlike in that it recognizes our very existence is a gift.[11]

The gathering of the church in regular patterns should create a safe place for play. Particularly, the great tradition as guiding belief and the tradition of mystery and encounter in the pre-pentecostal and pentecostal churches creates this playground. From time to time, though, we must reclaim the playground from controlling impulses of leadership. Sometimes misguided missiological motivations baptize too much of the larger world culture in which the local church is embedded.

Pleasure and joy are gifts in common to being in a body, the shared human experience sustained by the Spirit everywhere. However, they can become negative when the underlying power is not known; thus the gifts become idols instead of gifts of being and are distorted or misshapen by the individual or community. The experience of drunkenness used in the cultic practices (Dionysian comes to mind) of antiquity (and even some today) are used as a bridging concept to show the power and contrast in being "filled with the Spirit" which results not only in joy-filled worship, but also in play that is, upon observation, likened unto the excess of drunkenness to the observing non-player.

Acts 2:13 relays, "But others jeered at the speakers, saying, 'They are drunk on new wine!'" Paul, in calling for orderly use of the charism of tongues in public worship, says, "So if the whole church comes together and all speak in tongues, and unbelievers or uninformed people enter, will they not say that you have lost your minds?"[12] Menzies argues that phrases within the New

11. Suurmond, *Word and Spirit*, 32–33.

12. 1 Cor 14:23.

Testament and Septuagint point to Jesus speaking in tongues in his praise inspired by the Spirit in Luke 10:21. This understanding is a speculation based on the apostolic interpretation of Psalm 16:8–11 applied to Jesus in Acts 2:25–28. These passages indicate (in Menzies's reading) that Jesus' earthly experience of his relationship with God the Father, through the Holy Spirit's mediation, included specifically his tongue used in jubilant, ecstatic, glossolalic praise.[13]

Addiction is often rooted in the experience of managing pain or a misuse of pleasure.[14] These are clear intersections where spiritual life and its effect upon the physical body converge. Addiction is where common grace experiences of play being abused, when linked with biological factors and genetic fallenness, can be turned into destructive practices. When one seeks to live only in common grace play, they lose sight of the empowerment to live differently in non-play life. This brings up the connection that what is experienced in the excess of addiction can be experienced in the fullness of the Spirit and then turned into empowerment instead of loss.

Play of the Spirit is different from common grace play in that the Spirit will always turn one back outward into non-play life. An addiction to the Spirit is impossible because God's very being is noncoercive love. Furthermore, the theophanic, love-rooted empowerment of and by the Spirit in play entails outward mission in the world, thus not allowing for the inward collapse of addiction. The Spirit-directed play will tear down walls and also replace the addiction to non-Spirit play with another stimulus, which has the built-in virtue of being able to freely enter into and out of a play state without harming the person.

While one can attempt to individualize and ignore the social holiness dimensions of the Spirit's work in play, when this occurs the play devolves into emotional tweaking of entertainment, removing the empowerment and wall-destroying action of play. It is beyond the scope of this writing to wrestle extensively with a fuller sense of the differentiation between entertainment and play.

13. Menzies, *Speaking in Tongues*, 50–53.

14. Haines, *Coming Clean*, 21–23.

They vary essentially in the active role of the player-participant and in the outward impact; one leaves play awakened and altered, whereas one leaves entertainment dulled. When Pentecostals do not develop and teach a theology of the Spirit of God at play in worship arts, they tend to enter an entertainment mode based only on an evangelical missional model for worship. This strips out the essential difference between Spirit-filled and open participatory worship theology and returns to the performance or entertainment of the high medieval Roman church where the congregation was largely silenced and excluded into observing the performance of the special players.[15]

3.2 Encourage Speaking in Tongues in Gatherings

Do not forbid anyone from speaking in tongues

— 1 Corinthians 14:39

Given what was said before, in order to cultivate speaking in tongues, pentecostals and charismatics must return to their welcoming of the other (in particular speaking in tongues) in worship and jettison evangelical respectability. First and foremost those who already have this gift must be encouraged to exercise it in order as based on Acts and 1 Corinthians 12–14 and as a prayer language out loud in times of communal prayer in planned worship and prayer gatherings. I wholeheartedly affirm Menzies's statement that "we need to account for the fact that speaking in tongues was well known, widely practiced, and generally held in high esteem in the early church."[16]

Prophetic words and modes are to be welcomed as well in the gathered worshiping community. Pentecostals need to be reminded that the growth curve arcs downward when the distinctiveness one has to offer through a radical openness to the public use of the gifts of the Spirit is lost for a prideful pursuit of affirmation from

15. Vondey, *Beyond Pentecostalism*, 147.

16. Menzies, *Speaking in Tongues*, 63.

those who are more captive to cultural acceptance. In short, mystical distinctiveness is inherently missionally powerful for those who are truly searching and responding (often unknowingly) to the Holy Spirit's drawing. The missional relevance of the seemingly irrelevant has to be rediscovered. Mystery bathed in the word and Spirit is perhaps the most relevant thing (along with provision for physical needs) that we can offer.

There is a "weird" which is bad, and there is a "weird" which, counterintuitively, is attractional. Speaking in tongues should be a spiritual gift, along with prophetic speech, that is encouraged, promoted, and not silenced by the gathered community in worship and prayer. Speaking in tongues is not tamable and feeds the holy imagination; this means that a pentecostal/charismatic liturgy planning should include intentional space for silence and the vocal response of the gathered community. This is important for traditioning its use in worship for those who have not sought the gift of speaking in tongues, nor experienced the play of non-cognitive language. People need to observe the play, be challenged by it, see the fog, and be lovingly encouraged to seek through it. Play of the Spirit in "tongues speech" has a beginning and an end; there is a crossing of the threshold into this new dimension.[17] Menzies, in interpreting an understanding of Paul's corrective restrictions of excessive and elitist use of tongues in Corinth, says, "It is evident that Paul would recognize the value of uninterpreted tongues on corporate worship as long as it is expressed communally, such as in concert prayer or praise, and not as the focal point of an isolated event. In other words, if our expression of tongues in the context of corporate worship does not disrupt or eclipse intelligible forms of address, such as proclamation, instruction, or prophecy, then I find it hard to believe that Paul would object."[18]

Welcoming speaking in tongues in the gatherings of the church would also point back to Acts, where it was in the context of gatherings for prayer that this gift was manifest as well. Praying in the Spirit and singing in the Spirit are both mentioned by Luke

17. Chan, *Pentecostal Theology*, 56.
18. Menzies, *Speaking in Tongues*, 118, 120.

and Paul in the New Testament. As Chan puts it, "When tongues are exercised continually as the language of prayer, they become the occasion for a new theophany and a new level of intimacy with God."[19]

It is the Spirit who desires to turn the gathered believers into a community of prophets. A church gathering is a place for a theophany to occur which can bring others into the prophetic experience and "tongues speech."

3.3 Teach the Sinful Idolatry of Language

Teaching about the idolatry of language, particularly for the Western, secularly privileged believer, must be more intentional and, ironically, academic in some ways. We should not seek to silence tongues, nor should we seek to silence the beneficial analytical parts of Western culture. We need to embrace postmodernisms in their critique of means of control. A lengthy analysis of tongues as the God-ordained, ultimate postmodern critique would be of great philosophical import, but is beyond the scope of this paper. To quote Suurmond again, "Glossolalia does not use an existing vocabulary, but it is not gobbledegook either. It is a playful way of communicating, comparable with abstract art or music. Glossolalia is a purposeless, unformed expression of the self in Word and Spirit, unhindered by rules of language and codes of behavior; it is an expression of a bond with God and other people which transcends barriers [of language]. . . . The gift of tongues is also an implicit criticism of any language that tries to 'capture' God."[20]

Speaking in tongues reveals God's nature both positively, what we can say God is *like*, and negatively, what we can say God is *not*. "God's 'strength' is grounded in babes and infants, symbols of vulnerability and play."[21] A Christology that is only "word"-oriented feeds into an overly Helenized way of being; to use colloquial faith

19. Chan, *Pentecostal Theology*, 77.

20. Suurmond, *Word and Spirit*, 156.

21. Suurmond, *Word and Spirit*, 35.

language, it is too "head-religion" oriented. A Spirit-Christology is playful.

Pentecostals, as has been well documented by others, have had an anti-intellectual bent. In part this was because the Western church in which it was birthed had lost the language of the mystical to speak about the unspeakable. Pentecostals found the Western church academy more apt to kill what it refused to think about or could not explain in any positive way. In contrast, "tongues speech" could fit into a form of mystical theology and experiences in the Eastern Orthodox Church's negative (apophatic) theology tradition. In my view, it is a literal embodiment, by the energies of the Spirit, of both positive and negative elements of theology. While the person is praying in tongues it is a form of "negative theology by negations. . . . The perfect way, the only way which is fitting in regard to God, who is of His very nature unknowable."[22] For the unfamiliar, that is to say we can only know God positively in God's condescending to us, but we cannot in our finite beings fully know God, except as a gift of encounter which is still limited, because we would cease to exist separately from God if there was a full union. Our positive theology is that in Christ we have seen the Father and he is our fullest picture of God outside of our experience. Mystical encounter in the Eastern Orthodox Church is not some cold, detached thing but rather an experience that brings one increasingly into a living relationship of love.

Teaching about language idolatry can focus on many different aspects. One such focus would be to include teaching about emotional liminality as a place where one can subdue the impulse of controlling language. It is in this place one may be most childlike to ask for the gift of the Spirit with specific gifts such as the prayer language of "tongues speech."[23] Speaking in tongues is "partial," and we need to be reminded of our "partialness" in order to remain dependent upon relationship and power outside of ourselves. This should be taught, meditated upon, and modeled in worship. The perfect is contrasted with the current use of spiritual

---

22. Lossky, *Mystical Theology*, 25.

23. Stronstad, *Prophethood*, 54.

gifts of tongues and prophecy, which are necessary in the pre-eschatological era as a reflection of only part of the whole. They are indeed necessary in their inherent reminders of the "not yet" aspect of life and era in God's time and plan. Speaking in tongues is a sign of our lack and incompleteness; tongues causes one to be aware of limits and the necessity of sustained relationship to experience life. The play of tongues empowers as well by revealing to us the vast extent of the true unknowns of being. Speaking in tongues resists domestication and simplistic drives to order and control our world, particularly through naming and language.

Naming is often thought of as an important aspect of liberation and recovering from victimhood thinking. However, naming is also an act of control that can enslave one again. If the gift is used and the play of it is continually renewed and entered into again, speaking in tongues allows a kind of naming that does not ensnare the victim as a new agent of division and breaks the possibility of a vicious cycle of oppressed becoming oppressor. When modern US pentecostalism is compared to its earlier Azusa days, we see that where speaking in tongues has decreased, the old divisions have increased.

"Tongues speech" should be also taught as a paradigm of death for those who are privileged. In it there is a chosen and paradoxical death to language and to will through regular use of language. This death forces the secularly empowered, the privileged, to face the death of their control through the means of discourse and its claim on their existence. To seek to receive the gift of speaking in tongues is to choose a downwardly mobile path by rejecting language always at the control of the speaker and for the speaker's privilege maintenance.[24] "The false self must die so that a person can be reborn with his or her true self. . . . Only when people face their mortality and thus recognize that they are creatures do they discover that they are grounded in the unbounded creator. Then in the Word and the Spirit they can become transparent to God who plays the game of love—following Jesus."[25]

24. Nouwen, *In the Name of Jesus.*
25. Suurmond, *Word and Spirit,* 137.

The death of language control and games is embraced in seeking, receiving, and speaking in tongues. Death does not have the last word in tongues speaking; however, it paves the way for a new mode of affirmation outside of the former modes rooted in division, suppression, privilege maintenance, and control. Speaking in tongues should be encouraged for this aspect alone, breaking the elitist idols in the church. "The Word becomes the Word of the elite who have to learn to write, to preach, to discuss. The word of dogma begins to justify the exclusion of those who think differently, a development which reached a climax in the Church of Rome in the last century in the pope's claim to infallibility."[26] We would add in fundamentalist and progressive claims to justice and righteousness too. The privileged can enter into solidarity with those who are suffering and are the "other" by means of consistent prayer in tongues. The privileged are also liberated from humanity-devaluing lies about others that they have believed. The play entered into in "tongues speech" enables one to get true identity in God's love and presence first and reorders all the false self-idols down to the very words we use to shape and control our circumstances and the circumstances of others. The cross is experientially embraced in speaking in tongues, as is the power of resurrection. As mentioned earlier, Spirit baptism is water baptism from the inside out and needs to be reentered again and again until the perfect comes (1 Cor 13:8–10).[27]

3.4 Create Environments Where Liminality Can Be Experienced

Leaders should create worship orders, environments, and liturgies where "tongues speech" is encouraged within bounds. "There are other expressions of speaking in tongues that appear to fall outside

26. Suurmond, *Word and Spirit*, 61.

27. "Love never ends. But if there are prophecies, they will be set aside; if there are tongues, they will cease; if there is knowledge, it will be set aside. For we know in part, and we prophesy in part, but when what is perfect comes, the partial will be set aside" (1 Cor 13:8–10).

of Paul's intended scope here [in 1 Cor 14:27–28 on limiting speaking in tongues in worship at Corinth]. These would include singing and, at times, praying in the Spirit (in tongues) in the context of corporate worship. The key here is that these expressions of tongues should not be disruptive of intelligible proclamation or teaching, should be subject to the leadership of the church, and thus should be done at appropriate times designated by church leaders."[28] This is something that we are losing with the shift of modern worship being formed more by missional theology than encounter-based theology. Most charismatics seem to have lost the ability, which perhaps they never truly had, to understand the role of art and music in shaping or limiting charismatic expression in the church. Lament and emotional liminality as possible in worship causes, "in the ritual setting [i.e., worship], participants [to] pass through pre-liminal, liminal, and post-liminal phases in which they step out of the expectation and structure of society into a 'betwixt and between' phase of possibilities and potentialities."[29] The pastor, liturgist, worship leaders, and planners all need to have a personal grasp of this through their own prayer life and worship experiences so that they may lead and pastor a gathered community into these experiences. Common grace play points to what also allows us to enter into marginal places where we open ourselves up to Spirit-led play in the gifts. "The gifts of grace are relational in the New Testament. So they cannot be detached from the relationship with the other, and they encourage the 'building up' of the community (1 Cor 14:12)."[30]

The Eastern Orthodox Church has a rich theological language which needs to be engaged with more fully. Several of our authors, such as Suurmond, have some basic engagement, but there is still more that can and should be done. In particular, speaking in tongues contains some clear intersections with mystical theology, and, more focused still, it gives mystical language to the ineffable by being in prayer practice ineffable. "Tongues

28. Menzies, *Speaking in Tongues*, 151.

29. Althouse, *Joel and the Spirit*, 267.

30. Suurmond, *Word and Spirit*, 170.

speech" is embodied liminality. As Daniela Augustine puts it, "*Xenolalia* and *glossolalia* have a sacramental function in the life of the Charismatic community, articulating the mystery of the union of the redeemed creation with its Creator and experiencing the in-breaking of the eschatological fullness of Christ in His Body."[31]

A gift is an unknown quantity until received or opened; in the case of tongues (glossolalia), it remains an unknown thing. The physical and spiritual come together in the act of speaking in tongues. Simon Chan simply states, "Baptism in the Holy Spirit [in the classical Pentecostal sense of initial physical evidence with speaking in tongues] . . . is nothing less than the revelation of the triune God."[32] This is defining tongues as a theophanic descent. However, as the prayer language is practiced by an individual, it has the ability, woven with contemplation, to be a negative ascent.[33]

Speaking in tongues in a limited way gives us a personal experience of the infinite and incomprehensible God. This is the mystical aspect of play. We might say play is the Pentecostal language for mystical encounter. In this way Pentecostalism, and "tongues speech" in particular, bridges the Western and Eastern churches. Tongues is a kind of embodied negative theology in prayer. It is at once a condescension of God and a language of negation that allows for ascent into a mystical union, what we are naming as that which can happen in true play, beyond performance. "God condescends towards us in the 'energies' in church He is manifested; we move towards Him in the 'unions' in which He remains incomprehensible by nature."[34]

So, for the new believer, the gift of tongues functions as a type of mystical onramp with an immediate sense of personal empowerment which liberates and informs non-play, non-mystical prophetic speech. The outward energies of God are being expressed through them. However, if one continues to pray in tongues, there is a transition into a spiritual journey that many pentecostals today

31. Augustine, "Empowered Church," 175.

32. Chan, *Pentecostal Theology*, 10.

33. Suurmond, *Word and Spirit*, 159–60.

34. Lossky, *Mystical Theology*, 39.

seem unaware of, yet there has been an attempt to speak of this ascent to union with God in Pentecostal and Charismatic circles since the beginning of the movement. The lack of language to describe this, in part because the Western church was so captive to enlightenment ways of speaking and separated from the Eastern Orthodox Church, has resulted in a loss of traditioning. Chan himself does not delve fully into this in his robust discussion of traditioning. The ongoing spiritual practice of "tongues speech" can result in a deeper liberation into the life of love through divine union. This brings the speaker to a place of engagement with the sins of humanity on another plane of being through a continued breaking down of control and "knowledge of good and evil" being reformed fully by divine and uncreated love.

An additional step to encourage speaking in tongues would be teaching and creating places for prayer to be practiced, which brings together the wrongly divided contemplative and charismatic traditions. Silence and tongues are connected in prayer and empowerment, as noted earlier. Churches with the facilities to do so should consider the reinvigoration of the prayer chapel. Experiences that move people out of non-play life into play, another way to speak of liminality, can be encouraged through personal retreats for the express purpose of prayer and listening. It is in these environments that people can learn to push beyond their normal view of life and enter cycles of contemplation and reception of spiritual gifts. This may take time and many encounters in order to move into a deeper charismatic phase of union with God.

In the group setting, art, and specifically music, has been shown to be of great power. This is a more active engagement of the Spirit in community, which we have addressed earlier in the discussion of common grace play of the Spirit. We will, however, spend a moment exploring this from another angle. The aesthetic experience is a common grace on-ramp into play, and when matched with the particularity of the Spirit of Creation, the very Spirit of Christ, it becomes a means of grace and encounter. "Pentecostal musicians in tune with the Spirit should likewise see themselves as musicians who play *in the Spirit*. The creative and spontaneous flow of music that connects the musician to God in a worship experience that is deep and unexplainable is the Spirit playing through them."[35] This kind of musician and musical worship leadership should be welcomed and cultivated in the churches.

Singing brings musicality to language beyond the normal patterns of tone in a given language. I believe when God spoke creation into being, God actually sang it into being. We think of the worship of heaven as something God passively takes in. I think this is quite wrong; God is singing, sustaining everything, and we are joining in the song, the play of the Father, Son, and Spirit. We start by singing to the Lamb, but soon we find that the Lamb has become the Bridegroom and the King and is singing with us. Again, Melissa Archer states, "As early pentecostals discovered singing in the Spirit (often in tongues) can be a means for the Spirit to sing a prophetic word in the midst of the worshipping community. . . . In many contemporary Pentecostal churches, this ritual of singing in the Spirit is seldom given space within the liturgy, yet perhaps a renewed understanding of it as a means for the Spirit to speak a prophetic word will lead to a retrieval of this Spirit-led liturgical activity."[36]

The use of music in worship calls us into an experiential encounter that can open us to a new level of liminal encounter. A Charismatic theology of encounter in worship is based on moving beyond the notes and rhythm to a meditative encounter. Colossians 3:16 points to this in corporate worship when it calls for a place for "spiritual songs." As Chan relates:

> A parallel phenomenon can be found in the Pentecostal practice of singing a short chorus over and over. Sometimes these choruses are derived from previously uttered "prophetic words."
>
> The Pentecostal ascetics also "sing in the Spirit" as mentioned by Paul and also Luke 10.21 of Jesus "rejoicing in the Spirit." Francis Sullivan has noted that this singing in the Spirit or singing in Tongues is remarkably similar

---

35. Archer, '*I Was in the Spirit*,' 318.
36. Archer, '*I Was in the Spirit*,' 315.

to what the ancients called the *jubilus*, of which there is a succinct description in Augustine. "What does it mean to sing in jubilation? It means to realize that you cannot express in words what your heart is singing. People who are singing, for example, during the harvest or the vintage or some other such ardent work, who have begun to exult with joy in the words of song, as if filled with such great joy that they can no longer express it in words, leave off the syllables of words and go into the sound of jubilation. . . . If you cannot express Him in words, and yet you cannot remain silent either, then what is left but to sing in jubilation, so that your heart may rejoice without words, and your unbounded joy may not be confined by the limits of syllables."[37]

This is known among Pentecostals today as one way people receive the gift of tongues; it lets the emotions be channeled into letting go of worry and other concerns to focus on the joy of God in Christ. It can be the holy laugh or the single-hearted focus on the joy of the unconditional love of God that allows for a mystical encounter through the exhausting of communicative language. Here some have received the gift of tongues in this joyful place of liminality. This is the other end of the spectrum from lament and grief for the world and brokenness expressed in prayer to a place of emotional focus or exhaustion that can also pour forth into "tongues speech" as an initial gift or response. These places where limits are reached and thresholds are crossed are best expressed in silence or "tongues speech."

If one is stuck in his or her faith, reengaging "tongues speech" creates an imaginative space of darkness, or (to use Western mystical language) tongues shifts from initial empowerment and experience of Divine Love for us, to being in the noncommunicative, frustrating, or even dead-feeling dark night of the soul. It sustains us in the break that occurs in all maturing Christians who cannot go back to the earlier stages of faith. There are rich resources to bolster the mystical encounter and its empowering work. In sum,

---

37. Chan, *Pentecostal Theology*, 84–85.

speaking in tongues can further be understood through the lens of negation.

3.5 Acknowledge the Need for Power

We have explored the notion of power as an outcome of engaging in play. Too often though we have only taught power without exploring the ways of play. Power in the church that is not rooted in play, and the love expressed in it, too often is twisted and becomes a new idol. There is real power, however, in the play of tongues that turns one into a prophetic sign, leading to new words and actions that challenge the givens around us. "The Spirit who drives us forward to a hope beyond history also drives us back into history, challenges us to take our historical existence with utmost seriousness."[38]

"Tongues speech" is a gift that bring us to a place of play with prophetic empowerment. But it is part of a kingdom that seeks the empowerment of all based on the superabundance of God. This power is manifest now. "In every case, not only in Pentecost, this baptizing with the Spirit, as the promise of the Father, is a clothing with power."[39] Yes, of course one must first go through death, crucifixion, before being conformed to Christ, but the promise of post-Easter power is real. This is where Pentecostals often break from most Protestants. There is affirmation of divine power expressed or working through love that brings new realities to bear on old ones this side of the eschaton. While many warnings of an over-realized eschatology are important, it is also important to understand that the current power of holy imagination and play is real, based on what one day will come in its fullness.

The power that is also sustained in tongues is the sense of "otherness." The church maintains power not only through identification, but also through differentiation, which at its best is for the purpose of blessing those who are its enemies. Retaining

---

38. Chan, *Pentecostal Theology*, 110.
39. Stronstad, *Charismatic Theology*, 57.

a sense of exile is difficult, as one is in an omnipresent culture. Because tongues cannot be assimilated they are the speech of exile, a language of resistance.[40] As such, they empower those who are privileged in a given culture to open themselves to exiles outside of the church's chosen exile. Finally, we can see that as Rom 8:22–26 indicates, there is strength accessed through the praying of the Spirit with "groans" and "sighs which cannot be uttered," but which God receives and acts upon by empowering us in the dark play of releasing brokenness and injustice to God. "Tongues speech" sustains the good news in the face of all other barriers to the creative word of God.

40. Smith, "Tongues as Resistance Discourse," 110.

Summary

It has been my goal to explore more connection or intersection between speaking in tongues with the developing Pentecostal theology which emphasizes play of the word and Spirit in communities (and persons). Play is received as gift by means of the gifts of the Spirit. Furthermore, we have looked at how play liberates and empowers through imagination and has common grace aspects in sport and aesthetic experience. We then specifically applied this lens to "tongues speech" and its play and prophetic dimensions. Speaking in tongues is the one gift which intrinsically maintains the otherness of God while empowering the person and persons in community; as such, it is a sustaining gift, resisting efforts to twist its power. "Tongues speech" sustains holy imagination, parable, and play. Finally, I have provided some teaching "handles" with which pastors and teachers can launch discussions and new experiences of worship.

Suggestions for Further Study

AREAS THAT HAVE ONLY been touched on where more intersectional work should be done specifically in regards to speaking in tongues include:

1. Philosophy of language analysis of speaking in tongues along with brain studies of people who are speaking in tongues. There is some limited research but little bridging with language philosophy.

2. Aesthetic philosophy of play. Some of our conversation partners have brought in Hans G. Gadamer's *Truth and Method* and Johan Huizinga's *Homo Ludens* discussion of play. When play becomes "being" in art, it is transformed in structure. This transformation makes play pure and detached from its players—or, indeed, they become its players. In this state it is permanent. Autonomy is the character trait of play. It is transformation over alteration into a structure that previously didn't exist. At this point the players cease to exist. The artist's, the performer's, and the player's identity ceases for those taking in the play, or more accurately being taken in by the play, and they ask, "What does it mean?" At this point, the knowledge of the art is communicated to the person.

3. Speaking in tongues as language of negation and the negative theology of the Eastern Orthodox Church.

4. Speaking in tongues in light of Wolfgang Vondey's *Beyond Pentecostalism: The Crisis of Global Christianity and the Renewal of the Theological Agenda.*

5. Gift theory.

6. Research on traditioning practices in pastoral theology and application.

Sources Consulted

Abraham, Shailbu. *Pentecostal Theology of Liberation: Holy Spirit & Holiness in the Society*. New Delhi: Christian World Imprints, 2014.

Albert, Eleanor. "Christianity in China." Council on Foreign Relations. Last updated October 11, 2018. https://www.cfr.org/backgrounder/christianity-china.

Alexander, Estrelda. *Black Fire: One Hundred Years of African American Pentecostalism*. Downers Grove: IVP Academic, 2011.

Alexander, Paul. *Pentecostals and Nonviolence: Reclaiming a Heritage*. Eugene, OR: Pickwick, 2012.

Althouse, Peter. "Betwixt and Between." In *Toward a Pentecostal Theology of Worship*, edited by Lee Roy Martin, 265–79. Cleveland, TN: CPT Press, 2016.

Anderson, Allan. *An Introduction to Pentecostalism: Global Charismatic Christianity*. Cambridge, UK: Cambridge University Press, 2004.

Archer, Melissa L. *'I Was in the Spirit on the Lord's Day': A Pentecostal Engagement with Worship in the Apocalypse*. Cleveland, TN: CPT Press, 2015.

Atkinson, William. *Baptism in the Spirit: Luke-Acts and the Dunn Debate*. Eugene, OR: Pickwick, 2011.

Augustine, Daniela C. "The Empowered Church: Ecclesiological Dimensions of the Event of Pentecost." In *Toward a Pentecostal Ecclesiology*, edited by John Christopher Thomas, 157–80. Cleveland, TN: CPT Press, 2010.

Bom, Klaas. "Heart and Reason: Using Pascal to Clarify Smith's Ambiguity." *Pneuma: Journal of the Society for Pentecostal Studies* 34.3 (2012) 345–64.

Boyd, Gregory A. *Seeing Is Believing: Experience Jesus through Imaginative Prayer*. Grand Rapids: Baker, 2004.

Brekke, Gregg. Review of *Signs and Wonders: Why Pentecostalism Is the World's Fastest Growing Faith*, by Paul Alexander. United Church of Christ, May 14, 2009.

Brueggemann, Walter. *The Practice of Prophetic Imagination: Preaching an Emancipating Word*. Minneapolis: Fortress, 2012.

———. *The Word Militant: Preaching a Decentering Word*. Minneapolis: Fortress, 2007.

Castelo, Daniel. "The Improvisational Quality of Ecclesial Holiness." In *Toward a Pentecostal Ecclesiology*, edited by John Christopher Thomas, 87–104. Cleveland, TN: CPT Press, 2010.

Chan, Simon. *Pentecostal Theology and the Christian Spiritual Tradition.* Eugene, OR: Wipf & Stock, 2000.

"Confession of Faith in a Mennonite Perspective." Mennonite Church USA, https://www.mennoniteusa.org/who-are-mennonites/what-we-believe/ confession-of-faith/.

Coulter, Dale M. "The Whole Gospel for the Whole Person: Ontology, Affectivity, and Sacramentality." *Pneuma: The Journal of the Society for Pentecostal Studies, 2nd ed.* 35.2 (2013) 157–61.

Crawford, Nathan. *Holy Imagination: Rethinking Social Holiness.* Lexington, KY: Emeth, 2015.

Crossan, John Dominic. *The Dark Interval: Towards a Theology of Story.* Niles, IL: Argus Communications, 1975.

Fee, Gordon D. *The First Epistle to the Corinthians.* Grand Rapids: Eerdmans, 1987.

Haines, Seth. *Coming Clean: A Story of Faith.* Grand Rapids: Zondervan, 2015.

Kärkkäinen, Veli-Matti. *The Spirit in the World: Emerging Pentecostal Theologies in Global Contexts.* Grand Rapids: Eerdmans, 2009.

Larkin, William J., et al. *Acts.* IVP New Testament Commentary 5. Downers Grove: InterVarsity, 1995.

Lossky, Vladimir. *The Mystical Theology of the Eastern Church.* London: Clarke, 1957.

———. *Orthodox Theology: An Introduction.* Crestwood, NY: St. Vladimir's Seminary Press, 1978.

Lyotard, Jean-Francois. *The Postmodern Condition.* Manchester: Manchester University Press, 1979.

Macchia, Frank D. *Justified in the Spirit: Creation, Redemption, and the Triune God.* Grand Rapids: Eerdmans, 2010.

Martin, Lee Roy, ed. *Toward a Pentecostal Theology of Worship.* Cleveland, TN: CPT Press, 2016.

McQueen, Larry R. *Joel and the Spirit: The Cry of a Prophetic Hermeneutic.* Sheffield, UK: Sheffield Academic, 1995.

Menzies, Robert P. *The Language of the Spirit: Interpreting and Translating Charismatic Terms.* Cleveland, TN: CPT Press, 2010.

———. "Pentecostal Theology and the Chinese Church." ChinaSource. Last modified January 21, 2015. https://www.chinasource.org/resource-library/blog-entries/pentecostal-theology-and-the-chinese-church/.

———. *Speaking in Tongues: Jesus and the Apostolic Church as Models for the Church Today.* Cleveland, TN: CPT Press, 2016.

Menzies, William W., and Robert P. Menzies. *Spirit and Power: Foundation of Pentecostal Experience: A Call to Evangelical Dialogue.* Grand Rapids: Zondervan, 2000.

Sources Consulted

Miller, Donald E., and Tetsunao Yamamori. *Global Pentecostalism: The New Face of Christian Social Engagement.* Berkeley: University of California Press, 2007.

Mittelstadt, Martin William. *Reading Luke-Acts in the Pentecostal Tradition.* Cleveland, TN: CPT Press, 2010.

Noel, Bradley Truman. *Pentecostal and Postmodern Hermeneutics: Comparisons and Contemporary Impact.* Eugene, OR: Wipf & Stock, 2010.

Nouwen, Henri J. M. *In the Name of Jesus: Reflections on Christian Leadership.* New York: Crossroads, 1989.

Pinnock, Clark H. *Flame of Love: A Theology of the Holy Spirit.* Downers Grove: InterVarsity, 1996.

Rees, Janice. "Subject to Spirit: The Promise of Pentecostal Feminist Pneumatology and Its Witness to Systematics." *Pneuma: The Journal of the Society for Pentecostal Studies* 35.1 (2013) 48–60.

Smith, James K. A. *Thinking in Tongues: Pentecostal Contributions to Christian Philosophy.* Grand Rapids: Eerdmans, 2010.

———. "Tongues as Resistance Discourse." In *Speaking in Tongues: Multidisciplinary Perspective*, edited by Mark J. Cartledge, 81–110. Eugene, OR: Wipf & Stock, 2006.

Stronstad, Roger. *The Charismatic Theology of St. Luke: Trajectories from the Old Testament to Luke-Acts.* 2nd ed. Grand Rapids: Baker Academic, 2012.

———. *The Prophethood of All Believers: A Study in Luke's Charismatic Theology.* Sheffield, UK: Sheffield Academic, 1999.

Studebaker, Steven M. *Defining Issues in Pentecostalism: Classical and Emergent.* Eugene, OR: Pickwick, 2008.

———. *From Pentecost to the Triune God: A Pentecostal Trinitarian Theology.* Grand Rapids: Eerdmans, 2012.

Suurmond, Jean-Jacques. *Word and Spirit at Play: Towards a Charismatic Theology.* Grand Rapids: Eerdmans, 1995.

Thiselton, Anthony C. *The Holy Spirit: In Biblical Teaching, through the Centuries, and Today.* Grand Rapids: Eerdmans, 2013.

Vondey, Wolfgang. *Beyond Pentecostalism: The Crisis of Global Christianity and the Renewal of the Theological Agenda.* Grand Rapids: Eerdmans, 2010.

Warrington, Keith. *Pentecostal Theology: A Theology of Encounter.* London: T. & T. Clark, 2008.

Watson, Kevin. "Wesley Didn't Say It: 'Personal and Social Holiness.'" May 20, 2013. https://kevinmwatson.com/2013/05/20/wesley-didnt-say-it-personal-and-social-holiness/.

Witherington, Ben, III. *Conflict and Community in Corinth: A Socio-rhetorical Commentary on 1 and 2 Corinthians.* Grand Rapids: Eerdmans, 1995.

Author Index

Author Index

Subject Index

Scripture Index

Scripture Index

Romans

1 Corinthians

Ephesians

Colossians

James

1 John